Making Sense of
English Usage

David Crystal

Chambers

Published 1991 by W & R Chambers Ltd
43–45 Annandale Street, Edinburgh EH7 4AZ

© David Crystal 1991

A catalogue record for this book is available from the
British Library

ISBN 0–550–18036–2

Typeset by Butler & Tanner Ltd, Frome, Somerset
Printed in England by Clays Ltd, St Ives plc

Contents

Preface

Before I began to write this book, I counted my collection of books and booklets on English usage: I discovered I had over 200 of them, with titles ranging from the coolly academic ('A Guide to English Usage') to the emotionally involved ('A Dictionary of Diseased English'). They ranged in size from a few dozen pages to nearly 1000 pages. They spanned a period of nearly 200 years. They included a spectrum of attitudes about English which, at one extreme, represented the greatest imaginable tolerance of change and variety, and at the other the greatest imaginable conservatism and prescriptivism. The problem was evident: faced with such a vast library of deeply-held and diverse opinion, how would it still be possible to say anything fresh or interesting about the subject?

I decided to use the title of the present series ('Making Sense of') as my guide, and to apply it literally. I would, I thought, try to write a short usage book which explained a little of what the fuss was all about. Having written and presented a number of series on English usage for the BBC, during the 1980s, and received several thousand letters from listeners for my trouble, I have learned that the majority of enquirers are not people seeking authority or reassurance; they are simply people interested in language, curious about language change, and puzzled about why things are happening in the way they are. They want explanations, first and foremost. And insofar as they do want some guidance, they want this delivered in a sensible and objective way, and not thrust down their throats. People are now consumer-literate. They are well used to being presented with a range of alternatives, and being allowed to make up their own minds. A usage book needs to reflect this *Which?* mentality.

Another important principle followed from this: that people should be able to learn from their experience of using a usage book. Traditionally, usage books are used like dictionaries – a question comes to mind (eg does one say *burned* or *burnt?*), and the user looks up the answer. Let's assume that the answer is clear, and the questioner is satisfied. Now what follows? Usually, nothing. There is a lull until the next usage problem emerges. And a few days or weeks later, our questioner encounters another issue (eg does one say *smelled* or *smelt*?). Without any general principle, the new bit of looking-up remains unrelated to the old, and the fact that the two issues are dealing with the same basic problem is not even noticed. Indeed, it does not have to be a new issue. People often complain that they keep looking up the *same* usage question, because they can never remember what the answer was when they looked it up the previous time.

This enormous waste of time and motivation can be resolved only in one way – by making it clear to the questioner what the general issues of English usage are. Our questioner needs to be told what is happening to the language which has caused the usage variation to arise, and this needs to be phrased in such a general way that the principle can be learned ('taken on board', as the current phrase is) and used in order to help solve future problems. Space needs to be devoted to describing not only the usage variation itself, but the factors which have led to it – insofar as they are known.

Ah, there's the rub. For with so many areas of English usage, the factors are not known, or indeed there are no factors there at all. Take the many cases of confusion between pairs of words (what some books call the 'confusibles') – such as *militate* and *mitigate* or *pathos* and *bathos* or *baleful* and *baneful*. There is no principle available here. If you mix words like these up, then you mix them up. Whatever the reason for the confusibleness of, say, *militate* and *mitigate*, this won't help you sort out your problem with *pathos/ bathos* or *baneful/baleful*. And the same goes for the hundreds of other confusibles in English, which clutter up the pages of so many usage books, and which also motivate the 'synonym essays' placed at the end of many entries in the larger dictionaries. The world of confusibles is a random world, full of chance developments in sound and meaning. I have not totally ignored this world: I have included a few confusibles in the present book, simply to illustrate this kind of problem. But otherwise I have steered well clear of them. The space is better devoted to those usage issues where there *are* some principles to be learned.

I'll identify these principles in the next paragraph. But first I must explain another major exclusion which accounts for the idio-syncratic character of the present book. I have not tried to intro-duce all the usage problems which relate primarily to social change. There are hundreds of such issues, to do with ethnicity, sexuality, class, politics, the media, and so on. Several pages could be devoted, for example, to the 'U' versus 'non-U' feelings which accompany changing usage patterns in such areas as table manners, toiletting, foodstuffs, and furniture. Here too there are no discernible principles to follow: whatever the relationship between, say, *toilet* and *lavatory*, once you have understood it you are no nearer understanding the relationship between, say, *lunch* and *dinner*. I therefore also largely ignore these topics, apart from allowing in a few famous examples to illustrate the nature of this domain. (I say 'largely' because there is in fact one major area which *is* capable of being discussed in a principled way – the issue of gender – and that issue is regularly addressed in the book.)

What does that leave, you might by now be thinking? In fact, a great deal. It leaves the whole domain of grammar, which is where the most frequently occurring usage issues lie. The chances of coming across the *baneful/baleful* issue are not great, most days of the week. But the chances of coming across the question of which pronoun to use, or which auxiliary verb, or which past tense form, are very great – indeed, as soon as you begin the process of constructing a sentence, you are faced with a series of usage questions to do with grammar. Another area which can be approached systematically is the way that major regional divergence has taken place, notably between American and British English. Developing a sense of the differences here is well worth while, as they are a major influence on current preferences and dislikes in usage. The nature of the systematic variations which differentiate spoken and written English provides me with a third area which rewards careful investigation, and the differences between formal and informal English constitutes a fourth. You will, accordingly, find my entries full of observations about variations in medium (spoken and written), status (formal and informal), and region (international and intranational). Lastly, over and above all this, I have included some examples of all the other main types of usage problem, as any respectable anthologist should do. For, in many ways, this book *is* an anthology - a personal collection of the famous, the fascinating, and the fringe, chosen with the same kind of quirky sentiment as will be encountered in any other anthology, whether it be of poetry, anecdotes, or Christmas carols. The topics have interested me, and it is my hope that they will also interest you.

Any study of grammatical usage has a penalty – the need to use grammatical terminology. I have kept this to a minimum, and indeed have no entries identified using grammatical labels. I put my information on 'split infinitive', for example, under the word *to*, and just use a cross-reference to help people who know that term to find out where to look. If you find the grammatical terminology unfamiliar, I have added a short Glossary at the back of the book, which contains all the grammar terms I use. Certain other terms I explain below.

Chief among these other terms are those referring to the usage book genre itself. In almost every entry, the issues which interest or worry people have come from the statements of grammarians and usage pundits themselves. Only one thing is certain in the world of usage – that as soon as the language begins to change, someone will be along to worry about it, or to condemn it. The bulk of the entries in my 200 books are pessimistic – wishing that matters were simpler, wishing that things wouldn't change – in short, wishing that language wasn't language. When I talk about the 'usage manuals' in my book, I am referring to the general tenor of this genre – the generally prescriptive bias which fuels the black-and-white statements about correctness and incorrectness which have been the cause of so much disquiet. Then, within this general tradition, there is a noticeable anxiety to try to keep the language pure, by retaining the essential features of earlier word meanings, avoiding external influences, and maintaining strict distinctions between grammatical constructions: this is the tradition I refer to as 'purist'. Another anxiety is to appeal to certain norms or canons of style, such as can be found practised by famous authors, and which often correspond to a widely-felt sense of appropriateness and excellence, though just as often they reflect no more than a critic's personal taste: this is the tradition I refer to as 'stylist'. I shall regularly refer to these attitudes in my entries, as a perspective for discussing the current linguistic situation.

I should perhaps emphasize, at this point, that I have no intention of tarring everyone with the same brush, by using these char-acterizations. It would be impossible to do justice to the insights of such usage giants as Fowler, Gowers, and Partridge, who dem-onstrated in their writing a genuine concern to explain and explore. Unfortunately, their insights have often been obscured by the mass of popular published prescriptivism which, in claiming to cater for the needs of the usage-insecure, actually feeds those insecurities. It is this aspect of the usage tradition that I wish to help counter, with this book.

As far as entry treatment is concerned, there is little to say. I have stayed with alphabetical order, rather than discuss issues thematically, because I think that most enquirers do approach a usage book with a specific word or phrase in mind. The alphabetical arrangement is letter-by-letter. To anticipate as wide a range of entry points to the book as possible, I have included a large number of cross references of the 'X see Y' type. There are also many end-of-entry cross references, to foster the sense of connections between usage issues which it is the primary purpose of this book to establish.

So, if you are hoping to use this usage book much as you might a confessional – coming to it burdened by feelings of linguistic guilt or inadequacy, you will remain dissatisfied at the end of it. I am giving out no absolution and no penances. If you come to it expecting to see a clear and authoritative statement about what is right and what is wrong, you will be highly disappointed. I am not speaking with the voice of infallibility, and I am not invoking any sanctions. If you are hoping for a comprehensive guide to the universe of usage, in all its manifestations, you will be thoroughly frustrated. This is a restricted and personal selection of what the language has on offer. But if your interests run deeper, if you are curious about the effects of linguistic change on language, and are looking for connections and explanations, and if you have previously found the stance of usage books unpalatable in their superior attitude and oversimplification – if, in a phrase, you simply want to 'make sense of English usage', then you should extract some satisfaction and, I hope, enjoyment from my approach, which I offer as a first step in getting to grips with this intriguing subject.

David Crystal

Pronunciation Guide

Vowels

i:	need	/niːd/
ɪ	pit	/pɪt/
i	very	/ˈvɛri/
ɛ	pet	/pɛt/
æ	pat	/pæt/
ʌ	other	/ˈʌðəʳ/
ʊ	book	/bʊk/
uː	too	/tuː/
u	influence	/ˈɪnfluəns/
ɒ	cough	/kɒf/
ɔː	ought	/ɔːt/
ɜː	work	/wɜːk/
ə	another	/ənˈʌðəʳ/
ɑː	part	/pɑːt/

Glides

eɪ	plate	/pleɪt/
aɪ	sigh	/saɪ/
ɔɪ	ploy	/plɔɪ/
oʊ	go	/goʊ/
aʊ	now	/naʊ/
ɪə	hear	/hɪəʳ/
ɛə	fair	/fɛəʳ/
ʊə	poor	/pʊəʳ/

Consonants

p	pit	/pɪt/
b	bit	/bɪt/
t	ten	/tɛn/
d	den	/dɛn/
k	cap	/kæp/
g	gap	/gæp/
ʃ	shin	/ʃɪn/
ʒ	pleasure	/ˈplɛʒəʳ/
tʃ	chin	/tʃɪn/
ʤ	budge	/bʌʤ/
h	hit	/hɪt/
f	fit	/fɪt/
v	very	/ˈvɛri/
θ	thin	/θɪn/
ð	then	/ðɛn/
s	sin	/sɪn/
z	zones	/zoʊnz/
m	meat	/miːt/
n	knit	/nɪt/
ŋ	sing	/sɪŋ/
l	line	/laɪn/
r	rid	/rɪd/
j	yet	/jɛt/
w	quick	/kwɪk/

ʳ indicates an 'r' pronounced only before a following vowel
ˈ precedes the syllable with primary stress

A

a, an

The rule governing the use of this pair of words seems straight-forward enough: *a* before consonants (*a car*) and *an* before vowels (*an arm*). Two points regularly appear in the usage manuals. The first concerns the situation before words beginning with *h*: some people use *an hotel* (pronounced /oʊ'tel/), for example, instead of *a hotel*. This possibility arises only in relation to words where the first syllable is unstressed, and where as a consequence the *h* isn't strongly sounded – other examples include *historian* and *habitual*. (There's no problem with such words as *history*, therefore, where the first syllable is stressed; these are always preceded by *a*.) *An* used to be the normal form of the article before *hotel* and the others; but since the turn of the century, this usage has been in steady decline. It is still used, however, especially by older people, and especially in writing. I've also heard it among some of the young upwardly-mobile, who have presumably been impressed by the usage of their seniors; but I doubt whether the general decline will be much arrested by a latter-day yuppy revival.

The second point to note is that some people can't stand the pronunciation of *a* as /eɪ/ (and a similar point is made about the pronunciation of *the* as /ðiː/ – 'thee'). The criticism isn't usually made when the contrast is motivated by the context, as in *I'd like /eɪ/ banana, not six bananas*. The irritation arises when there seems to be no need for any emphasis at all, as in *There's /eɪ/ new film at the cinema this week* or *That's /ðiː/ latest news from ITN*. It's a mannerism which is very common in formal American speech. In Britain, broadcasters tend to receive the brunt of the criticism, because (ironically) by attempting to speak clearly and slowly they readily slip into using the long vowel. Sports commentators also use the pronunciation as a 'delaying' tactic while they wait for an action to take place. It apparently drives some radio listeners up the wall.

ability

Which preposition can be used after this word? Standard usage prefers *in* before a noun (*Fred has great ability in the long jump*); but you'll sometimes hear *for*, and I've occasionally heard *at*. Before a verb, the usual preposition is *to* followed by the infinitive (*Fred has the rare ability to make friends easily*). When people want to emphasize the duration of an activity, I've often heard them use the *-ing* form of the verb: *Fred has the rare ability for/of making friends easily*. However, usage critics worry about these constructions, especially if they appear in formal writing. The uncertainty arises partly because there is quite an overlap between the meanings of the various prepositions, and partly because different prepositions follow words of closely related meaning (compare *capable of* and *capacity for*). It's not surprising that people tend to muddle them up, therefore, and that consistency of practice can be difficult to achieve.

about

About, *around* and *round* are all words which specify location in space or on a surface, relative to a focal point, so it's not surprising that people vary in their usage. *About* generally indicates an indefinite set of directions or positions in the vicinity of a point: *Newspapers were scattered about the bedroom*; *There are wolves about*. *Around* and *round* have similar ranges of meaning, but as well as an indefinite meaning (*standing (a)round*) they sometimes express a definite direction or position (often the complete encirclement of a point, as in *(a)round the corner/ clock/world* ...). They are often interchangeable, with a bias in British English towards *round* and in American English towards *around*, for the senses concerned with movement in a specific direction.

For the sense of 'approximately', more formal British usage prefers *about* to *around*: *about mid-day/10 pounds*. Many older speakers consider the latter to be an Americanism, and penalize it accordingly. Both British and American speakers use *about* informally in the senses of 'concerning' and 'nearly': *a film about fishing*; *I'm about ready*. *Round about* is also used informally, especially in British English, for extra indefiniteness of either quantity or location: *We stopped for a drink round about 11 o'clock/ Stratford* ...

The issue here, in short, is partly regional, with British and

American speakers among those who differ in their preferences, and partly stylistic, with people sensing that the words are not the same in their formality. The situation is not stable, because American usage is gradually influencing British and other regional varieties.

above

The above, *cf above*, *the above comments*, and other such locutions are used to refer to what has already been mentioned in written discourse (usually not too far back). The corresponding use of *below* refers to material mentioned later in the discourse. These usages are common in academic, business, and legal writing, but they are often considered awkward or stilted in other contexts, and are usually avoided in popular writing. They are especially thought to be inappropriate if used in writing intended to be read aloud (such as a speech or a news broadcast), where such forms as *earlier* and *later* would not attract notice. The use of *above* and *below* for cross-reference is one of the ways in which written and spoken discourse differ in their methods of organization.

absolutely

This is widely heard as a single-word response, as an intensive form of 'yes'. It was once largely restricted to American English, but British speakers have been coming out with it frequently in recent years. This won't endear them to purist critics of language, who object to the word being used in this way. The critics claim that it is misleading to use a word which can express such senses as 'perfect' and 'unconditional' in contexts where these meanings are not intended. However, there's no evidence to suggest that listeners are confused by these other meanings when they hear the word as a response.

Absolutely shows an interesting shift in its stress pattern as it moves about the sentence. When it's put at the end of a sentence, or after the word it modifies, the main stress is on *lute*: *I agree abso'lutely*; *Abso'lutely!*). When it precedes the word it modifies, the main stress is usually on *ab* (though the other stress pattern is sometimes heard), as in *I 'absolutely agree*, *You're 'absolutely right!*. (Compare the stress shift at **adverse**.)

acoustics

In its sense of 'the scientific study of sound', this word takes a singular verb and no article (*Acoustics is a fascinating subject*). In its sense of 'the total effect of sound in an enclosed space', it takes a plural verb, and the definite article (*The acoustics in the hall are marvellous*). This is one of several nouns ending in *-ics* which can be used in both a singular and a plural way (others include **politics** and **statistics**).

act

As countable nouns, *act* and *action* are sometimes inter-changeable. *Act*, however, emphasizes what is done, rather than the process of doing, and is especially applicable to a specific brief deed or performance by an individual. *Action* is more likely to be used when process or function are stressed, and when performance is complex or long-term. The language also con-tains many fixed phrases, where only one of these terms can be used, such as *an act of war/violence/love* ... (never **an action of ...*), *Actions speak louder than words*. There is also an interesting modern use which will attract criticism if used in formal writing: *I want a piece of the action* (ie of the most exciting activity). Criticism is also made of *act* when followed by an adjective. This is generally felt to be nonstandard in Britain, though it is much more acceptable in American English: *He's acting crazy*. The standard equivalent uses a following adverb: *He's acting stupidly*.

ad

This abbreviated form of *advertisement* is normal in informal American English speech. Its use is increasing in informal British English, where it seems to be replacing *advert*, but not without objection from those who find all Americanisms repugnant. *Ad* in Britain is already standard in certain fixed phrases, such as *want ads*.

AD

In formal usage, there is a long-standing convention to put *AD* before the date, which is always a specific year, rather than a century: *She died in AD 1000* (the *in* being generally omitted in American English). Informally, it is often used like *BC*, which always follows the date, and which may be applied to any specified period: *in the twelfth century AD*. Here the meaning is loosely 'after Christ', rather than literally *anno Domini*, in the year of the Lord'.

It should also be noted that, with increased attention being paid these days to the sensitivities of non-Christian believers, some writers make use of *CE* for 'Common Era' instead.

adverse

An interesting feature of this word is the way its stress pattern alters, depending on where it occurs in the sentence. Followed by a noun, *ad* usually carries the main stress: *'adverse criticism.* When the word is used after the verb, and without a following modifier, *verse* is stressed: *The circumstances were extremely ad'verse.* (Compare the stress shift at **absolutely**.)

admit

In the sense of 'let in', the usual prepositions following this verb are *to* and *into*: *That ticket will admit you (in)to the cinema.* In the sense of 'allow as true or valid', the preposition is *of*: *The statement doesn't admit of any other interpretation*, but here the *of* is often omitted these days. Some people replace *of* by *to,* in this context (presumably because *to* is so commonly used after *admit* elsewhere), but this usage is often criticized by those who use *of*. Similarly, in the sense of 'confess', there is variation over the use of *to*: you will find both *He admitted robbing the bank* and ... *to robbing the bank*. This variation is less likely, however, when the verb governs a noun. Here, the use of *to* is unusual: *She admitted her error*.

affect

People often mix up *affect* and *effect* in writing, because they are similar both in meaning and pronunciation. An extra complication is that both words may be used as verbs and as nouns. *Affect* is more commonly used as a verb, and *effect* as a noun. The usual meaning of *affect* as a verb is 'bring about a change in' (*Her attitude affected me greatly*), though the verb does have a few other uses (such as 'pretend to feel', in *He affected indifference*). The noun use of *affect* is rare, and is restricted to the context of psychology, where it means 'strong feeling, emotion': *the study of affect*. The adjectival use is similar: *the study of affective behaviour in humans*. The usual meaning of *effect*, as a verb, is 'cause' (*How shall we effect some economies?*), though this is relatively formal and uncommon. The everyday use of *effect* is as a noun, where it means 'result' (*The effect of passing her exams was remarkable*) or 'influence' (*She had a great effect on me*). The most common confusion is with this last use, where the corresponding verb would be *affect*: *She affected me greatly*.

after

After is used in Standard English both as preposition (*after the bus*) and conjunction (*after he left*, ...). In expressions of time, it is sometimes used informally as an adverb, in the sense of 'afterwards': *Do it after!*; *They came in soon after*. In formal speech or writing, *afterwards* would be preferred.

An interesting use of *after* occurs in Irish English – and to some extent in Welsh English – where it is used as part of the verb phrase to signal such meanings as recency and habitual activity: *I'm after writing to my brother*.

afterwards

See **after**

agenda

While originally *agenda* was felt to be the plural form of *agendum*, these days it is used as a singular noun, taking a singular verb: *The agenda is on your table*, *Have you an agenda?* A regular plural has been formed: *agendas*. This is one of several nouns with a Latin or Greek etymology where there has been controversy over which singular or plural form to use (compare **data**, **errata**, **stratum**). The controversy seems largely over in the case of *agenda*, however, with only the most conservative of usage manuals arguing in favour of *agendum*.

aggravate

In the sense of 'make worse', this word has never attracted criticism: *His actions aggravated the situation*. However, usage manuals have long been worried about the way this verb has moved away from its earlier meanings, and come to mean 'annoy': *Don't aggravate her any further!*. It is now extremely common in this sense, especially in informal speech. It is a tribute to the persistence of the purist tradition that, although the word has been used in this way for over 300 years, criticisms continue to be made of it. (Compare the etymological criticisms made of **anticipate**, **decimate**, **deprecate**.)

ago

Standard English uses the simple past tense form with *ago*: *I saw him six years ago*. Very occasionally in informal speech, the *have* form of the verb may be heard, especially when the *ago* phrase is something of an afterthought (*Yes, I've seen him – six years ago*). There is no difficulty over using *should/would have*, though: *I should have kicked him out six years ago* is universally acceptable.

The standard conjunction following *ago* is *that*: *It's three weeks ago that John came home*. *Since* is often used in informal speech and writing (*It's three weeks ago since the accident happened*), but this attracts criticism in usage manuals. Traditional grammarians point to the different 'direction' of the meanings of *ago* and *since*, and argue that their simultaneous use is contradictory – *ago* pointing away from the present, *since* pointing towards the present. The traditional recommendation would be either to use the *that* construction or to drop *ago* altogether: *It's three weeks since that happened*. The widespread use of *since*, however, suggests that, as so often happens, the processes of language change and the dictates of logical reasoning are going their separate ways.

agree

There is a variety of prepositional use following this verb. We normally agree *with* someone, and agree *to* something. With an impersonal subject, *with* is used: *This lifestyle agrees with me*, *This book agrees with that book*. In the sense of 'come to an arrangement' we find *about* (*Let's agree about that*) and *on* (*We've agreed on a good price*), though *on* is sometimes omitted, especially in British English (*We've agreed a good price*). *Upon* is also found, especially when the preposition occurs at the end of a sentence (*That's what we agreed upon*), where it contributes extra rhythmical weight. There is an interesting 'official' use of *agree* with the direct object in British English: *The tax inspector has agreed our claim*; *The wage claim was agreed by the management*. This last usage is sometimes condemned as unnecessary 'jargon' by those who feel the traditional use of the preposition should be retained.

ain't

This form has been a focus of critical attention for many decades, and its use arouses strong feelings in educational contexts. Its use in writing or formal speech is unequivocally condemned, unless a special effect (such as humour) is intended, or the sentence has a fixed, idiomatic structure, as in the case of *Things ain't what they used to be*. It is nonetheless widely used in colloquial speech, especially in American English, as a substitute for *aren't*, *isn't*, *hasn't* and *haven't*. All are considered nonstandard by educated speakers, with the *have* substitutions attracting the greatest criticism: *I ain't got nothing*.

Ain't I, while still condemned, is sometimes felt to be slightly less heinous – but only because the alternative forms have themselves attracted criticism. *Aren't I* is often felt to be awkward (*Aren't I having any?*), and has been attacked by some grammarians on the grounds that it misleadingly suggests a corresponding form **I are*. The use of *am I not* is very formal, and is often considered affected or stilted. *Amn't I* has no currency, other than in occasional jocular use and in some dialects (notably, in Irish and Scots English). In colloquial speech, *aren't I* is the informal norm in educated British English; forms with *ain't* are widespread in informal educated American English.

all

All can occur with both singular and plural verbs, depending on whether a countable or uncountable noun is present or understood: *All human life is precious* vs. *All (tables) are taken*. The use of *of* before the definite article, in such phrases, is optional: *all (of) the tables*. It is usually included in American English, and omitted in British English, especially in writing.

An adverbial use of *all*, as in *I'm not all that interested*, is common in informal speech or writing, but would attract criticism in formal contexts. There is also an increasing use of *all* as a direct modifier of nouns and adjectives (usually joined to these forms with a hyphen): *all-purpose*, *all-powerful*, *all-England final*. (See also **already**, **alright**, **altogether**.)

already

In Standard English, *already* is clearly distinguished from *all ready*, both in its written form (as here) and in speech (a strong stress on *all*; a weak stress on *al-*). The contrast in meaning can be illustrated from such a pair of sentences as: *They are already in the house* (ie they have just arrived) and *They are all ready in the house* (ie everyone is ready).

The use of *already* with the simple past tense is common in informal American speech, and becoming so in British English:

She already went. Formal English prefers the *have* form of the verb: *She has already gone.* Many people feel *already* to be somewhat more informal in final position in the sentence (*She has gone already*), and this is definitely so in the case of the emphatic form used by Jewish speakers, as in *I've given it to him, already* (where it means something like 'I'm telling you'). (See also **yet**.)

alright

'It's all wrong to write alright, all right?' Despite the fact that the single-word spelling has been in use for over a century (and etymologically is known from the 12th-century), it is widely corrected by teachers, book editors, and others when it occurs in formal writing. Not everyone is against it, though. Some commentators in fact have argued that it would be a good thing to distinguish between *alright* and *all right*, in much the same way as the spelling distinction between *already* and *all ready* reinforces a contrast of meaning (see **already, altogether**). For example, in *The papers are all right, alright?*, the first usage means 'totally correct' and the second means 'OK'. *Alright* is increasingly common, presumably because of the influence of *altogether*, *already*, and *almost*.

also

Many writers avoid using *also* as a connective word in the sense of 'and', presumably because they do not like the looseness of the construction, which is typical of spoken syntax: *Mary studied French and German, also Russian and Latin.* The use of *and also* in this context attracts no criticism, though the repetition of *and* might then prompt an alternative formulation (such as *in addition to*). A similar reluctance is sometimes observed over the use of *also* to begin a sentence: *The journey was very long. Also, the train was uncomfortable.* However, most writers see no problem with this construction.

alternative

The traditional attitude in grammar books has been to restrict this word to contexts where a choice between only two items is involved. In this tradition, *There were two alternatives* is unproblematic, but *There were three (or more) alternatives* is disallowed. The objection is based on etymological reasoning: because *alternative* derives from the Latin word *alter*, meaning 'other of two', purist critics think it should retain that sense in modern usage.

However, there is no obvious alternative way of expressing 'other of more than two', and people do not seem to think that the distinction between 'two' and 'more than two' is important. The more inclusive sense is widely encountered, therefore, and has been attested in formal writing since the mid-19th century, especially when an unspecific sense is being expressed: *There were several alternatives*. However, for older people, and for those they influence, the purist influence is difficult to shake off, and usage books will often still be seen to object to the extended sense, especially in writing and formal speech, and especially when preceded by a numeral: *There were four alternatives*. (See also **dilemma**.)

although

Although and *though* are often interchangeable: *I went to the party, (al)though I wasn't well*; *(Al)though I wasn't well, I went to the party*. *Though* is the more colloquial form, and tends to occur when the clause it introduces is in second position in the sentence; *although* is preferred with clauses in first position. *Though* can be also used in certain constructions where *although* cannot go: *Late though she was* ...; but not **Late although she was* .... The distinction between the two forms has not attracted much critical attention in usage manuals. However, the manuals do come down hard on the use of *altho* and *tho* as informal spellings (sometimes followed by an apostrophe), and recommend that they should never be used in formal writing, and preferably not in informal writing either.

altogether

When used before the word it modifies, the main stress is on the first syllable: *You're 'altogether wrong*. When used after the word it modifies, or in final position in the sentence, the main stress is on the syllable *ge*: *There were 50 alto'gether*. A clear distinction is made in writing between this form and *all together*, and any confusion would be considered a sign of lack of education. *All together* always applies collectively, in the sense of physical or metaphorical unity: *The people were standing all together*. The meaning of *altogether* is 'completely' or 'in all'.

am
See **ain't**

amend
Amend and *emend* are commonly confused, because of their similarities in both meaning and pronunciation. *Amend* is the more general term, meaning to 'alter', 'correct', 'improve': *He amended his ways, I'll amend what I said.* *Emend* has the restricted meaning of 'improving a text by critical editing'. The corresponding nouns are *amendment* and *emendment*. There is an intransitive use of the verb *amend* only: *When will he amend, I wonder?*, where the sense is 'reform'.

among
There is a long-established tradition in usage manuals which attempts to maintain a clear distinction between the uses of *among* and *between*. Because of its etymology, *between* is recommended as the word to use when only two items are to be distinguished: *Look at the difference in height between John and Alec*; for more than two, *among* is recommended. However, the realities of usage present a more complex situation. *Between* is often used for more than two, if the items are considered individually: *The prize was divided equally between the seven of us.* *Among* would be more likely in a collective (and often vaguer) context: *The prize was divided among all the workers.* This is by no means a modern development: as the *Oxford English Dictionary* points out, *between* has been used in relation to more than two entities from the earliest recorded times.

Amongst is widely considered a somewhat old-fashioned variant of *among*, but some speakers still regularly use it, and some say they do in fact prefer it in formal contexts. On the whole, its frequency of use seems to have markedly reduced in recent years, though it still has considerable currency in several regional dialects. (See also **whilst**.)

amongst
See **among**

amount
Standard English makes a distinction between *amount* and *number* in terms of whether they occur with uncountable ('mass') or countable nouns. *Amount* goes with an uncountable noun: *I*

spent a large amount of time; I'll have just a small amount of cake. *Number* goes with a countable noun: *I spoke to him a number of times*; *I ate a number of cakes*. In informal speech, though, people sometimes use *amount* with countable nouns: *the amount of times*, *any amount of tables*. This usage is universally considered by usage manuals to be nonstandard. A glance at the dictionary definitions of the two words will show that there is no important difference of meaning between them, but failing to maintain the grammatical distinction is generally taken to be a sign of carelessness or lack of education.

and

Several generations of people have been taught that it is bad style to begin a written sentence with one of the coordinating conjunctions – *and*, *but*, *or*. The main role of these conjunctions, according to the traditional conception of grammar which derives from Latin and Greek, is to link 'lower-level' parts of a sentence (words, phrases, and clauses), and not sentences themselves. However, it is not difficult to find many cases of authors using these conjunctions effectively at the beginning of a sentence. Thomas Macaulay, for example, presents a clear contrast in meaning in the following extract from *The History of England*, which would be less dramatic if the constructions were placed within the same sentence:

> There were gentlemen and there were seamen in the navy of Charles the Second. But the seamen were not gentlemen; and the gentlemen were not seamen.

Modern stylistic manuals, therefore, are less likely to condemn the usage out of hand, but it still attracts a great deal of criticism from those who were taught to avoid it. In everyday speech, of course, *and* is the most commonly used connecting word, and you will frequently hear sentences beginning in this way. It is in writing that the over-use of *and* is commonly criticized, especially by teachers, who see it in the written work of their children from a very early age, and who try to promote the alternative use of more sophisticated connecting words such as *also*, *moreover*, and *however*.
(See also **try**.)

anticipate

There is no problem over the use of this verb in the sense of 'act in advance' or 'forestall', as in *We anticipated the trouble by blocking the road*. However, some people claim they avoid using the word in the general sense of 'expect' or 'look forward to', as in *I'm anticipating his arrival next Friday*, and prefer to use a verb such as *expect* in this context. Critics argue that *anticipate* sounds unnecessarily cumbersome and pompous in this sense; it also moves away from its original etymological meaning in Latin (*ante-* 'before' and *capere* 'take'). However, the extension of meaning involved is a natural one, and has been attested since the 18th century; its widespread modern use does not seem to have resulted in confusion or ambiguity. (See also **aggravate**, **decimate**, **deprecate**.)

anxious

In the general sense of 'feeling anxiety', *anxious* may be followed by either *for* or *about* when referring to persons or personalized notions: *I was anxious for/about him/his welfare*. *About* is preferred when the reference is to objects: *I was anxious about the things in the car*. When the sense is 'causing anxiety', the preposition is *for*: *That was an anxious time for all of the family*. The informal sense of *anxious* as 'eager' may also involve a construction with *for* (*I'm anxious for you to come*), but the use of *that* is more common (*I'm anxious that you should come*). Purists disapprove of the extension of meaning to 'eager', on the grounds that the word in Latin meant 'troubled in mind', and argue that usage should be restricted to contexts of 'worry'. However, the development in sense has been attested since the early 18th century, and is now common.

any

In interrogative and negative constructions, there are several complex nuances of usage over the use of *any* compared with *some*. Both *Have you got some?* and *Have you got any?* are possible, but in the former case there is a more positive implication (the answer is more likely to be *yes*), and in the latter case a negative implication (the answer is more likely to be *no*). In the explicitly negative form, *any* is the expected usage (*He hasn't got any*, with *He hasn't got some* being very unlikely). Similarly, *I haven't got any money* does not have a corresponding form *I haven't some money*, though there is a more formal alternative, *I have no money*. There is also a very informal use of *any* in the sense 'at all', in negative and interrogative constructions: *That didn't help any*; *Did he move the piano any?* This is especially common in American English, where it contrasts with *some*: *That helped some* (meaning 'somewhat'). (See also **anymore**, **anyone**, **anyplace**, **anyway**, **either**, **some**.)

anymore

The writing of this locution as a single word is common in American English; British English prefers to use separate words: *any more*. In standard informal speech, it is used only in negative or interrogative constructions: *He doesn't live here anymore*; *Does he live here anymore?*. Some regional dialects, especially in the USA, also use the form in declarative statements (*He likes her anymore*, meaning 'He still likes her'), but there is no sign of this construction coming into Standard English.

anyone

Anyone/anybody and *someone/somebody* display similar nuances of implication as are illustrated for *any/some*. In addition, a distinction should be noted between '*anyone* ('any person') and '*any* '*one* ('any one person'), the latter having strong stresses on both words.

A long-standing controversy exists over the appropriate pronoun to use in certain types of sentence, where *anyone* is subject: *Anyone can do what – wants*. To use the pronoun *he* in a generic way, including both males and females, can lead to ambiguity, and since the 1960s this usage has attracted criticism for its male bias. On the other hand, the use of *she* in this context sounds odd and possibly insulting. To use *he or she* avoids any charge of sexism (though some insist it should be *she or he*), but the combined form is widely felt to be extremely awkward and unidiomatic. For such reasons, the use of *they* (and corresponding forms, such as *their* and *them*) is now commonly employed as a solution to the problem: *Anyone can sit where they like, can't they?*.

Unfortunately, that is not the end of the story. Although this construction has been in English for a long time, it upsets the traditional grammarian, who wants the singular sense of *anyone* to be matched by a singular pronoun or verb. In the days before the sexism issue became prominent, *he* was therefore recommended as the safest course of action in formal speech and writing. Today, *they* is the usual solution in informal contexts, because it avoids the sexism dilemma. This dilemma has not been resolved in formal contexts, however, where people sensitive to this issue usually resort to rephrasing their sentence. (See also **everyone, nobody, people, somebody**.)

anyplace

This is one of a set of words (others are *everyplace, noplace, someplace*) found only in informal usage, especially in American English: *I couldn't see it anyplace*. Formal usage prefers *anywhere*. In informal writing, it is sometimes found as two words: *any place*.

anyway

'*Anyway* and '*any 'way* (with strong stresses on both words) are interchangeable only in the sense of 'in any manner': *Do it anyway* (or *any way*) *you want*. When the sense is 'in any case' or 'at any rate', only *anyway* is possible: *He objected, but she went anyway*. When the sense is 'any course of action', only *any way* is possible: *Any way we choose will involve danger*. The form *anyways* is common in informal American English and in some regional British dialects. (See also **someway**.)

appendix

In its medical sense, the plural is the regular form, *appendixes*. In the sense of 'supplementary material at the end of a book', the traditional plural is *appendices*. The regular ending is now increasingly used here, though not as yet in formal or specialized contexts. However, the history of English shows many examples of irregular forms being replaced by regular ones (a process called *analogy*), and it is likely that in due course the same thing will happen to this word. (See also **index**.)

aren't

See **ain't**

around

See **about**

as

Several *as* constructions are potentially ambiguous. A sentence such as *She left as I asked a question* could be interpreted in either a temporal or a causative sense: 'She left at the same time as I asked a question' or 'She left because I asked a question'. As a consequence, many people consciously choose *because* rather than *as* when expressing the latter sense. Another case is *She likes reading as much as Jim*, which could mean 'as much as she likes Jim' or 'as much as Jim likes reading'. It is this potential ambiguity which prompts some people to use subject forms of pronouns instead of object forms in such sentences: for example, *She likes Jane as much as I (do)* vs. *She likes Jane as much as (she likes) me*. (For the *I* vs. *me* issue, see **I**, **like**, **than**.)

In positive comparisons, a double use of *as* is required: *It's as big as a tree*. In negative comparisons, usage manuals prescribe *so ... as* (*It's not so big as a tree*), but *as* is still widely used. *So* is never possible in the positive construction: we do not say **It's so big as a tree*. There are also several markedly informal uses of *as*, such as *I'm not sure as I will* (where *as* replaces *that* or *if*), and *I'm not sure as to whether I should go* (where formal English would remove the *as to*).

(See also **but**, **far**, **like**, **such**.)

at

The contrast between *at*, referring to a point, and *in*, referring to an area, is often lost when dealing with locations of uncertain size or importance. An encyclopedia, for example, would say *She died in London*, where there is no doubt as to the status of the place; but it might say either *She died at Holyhead* or *... in Holyhead*. Someone from Holyhead (such as myself), who knows it as an area, would instinctively expect *in*; someone for whom the town was merely a point on a map would, just as instinctively, expect *at*. Similarly, the BBC News would say *There has been a fire at Little Swapping in Wiltshire*, but someone who lives nearby would say *There's been a fire in Little Swapping*. The problem becomes significant when we are referring to locations in a foreign country, and where a major city might inadvertently be referred to as *at*.

ate

See **eat**

averse

Both *from* and *to* have been used after this word from as early as the 17th century. Those who argue in favour of *from* use an etymological argument: *a* in Latin meant 'away', and this meaning should continue to be reflected in the English preposition. Those who argue in favour of *to* point to the similarity in meaning between *averse* and *hostile*, *contrary* and other such words, which are followed by *to*. When etymology is set against analogy in a straight fight, the latter invariably wins. Today, *averse to* is the accepted form, with *averse from* rarely encountered. The same point applies to the noun *aversion*, which is principally used with *to*, less often with *for* and *towards*, and rarely with *from*.

await

See **wait**

awful

This adjective, and the corresponding adverb *awfully*, has been used as a general word of disapproval since at least the beginning of the 19th century, and is especially common in conversational English: *It's an awful book*. Its use as an intensifying word is also attested from that time: *an awful row*; *an awfully good play*. However, many people do not like to use the word in these contexts in formal speech or writing. You would be most unlikely to hear either the adjective or the adverb on the BBC News, for instance, unless in a quotation. The older use of *awful* ('causing a feeling of awe') is now restricted to literary, religious or other special contexts.

B

back

The construction *in back of*, meaning 'behind', is an American English usage; it has a colloquial variant *back of*, which is increasingly common in US speech. Despite the parallel between *in back of* and *in front of*, there is a reluctance to use the construction in formal writing, *behind* being preferred. The nearest British English equivalent is *at the back of*.

Usage manuals criticize the construction *back again* when it is used without any special stress on *again*. *Again*, the critics say, is felt to be redundant in a sentence such as *He gave it back again to the lady*, unless the implication is that the giving-back has taken place at least once before. They would recommend instead *He gave it back to the lady*. However, people often combine words of similar meaning in English, especially when they want to clarify a point or increase the emphasis being placed upon it, and *back again* is accordingly often used, both in speech and writing.

bacterium

Bacterium tends to be found only in specialist use; the term which has achieved popular recognition is the plural form *bacteria*. However, people who are not so familiar with the real singular form often use *bacteria* as a singular as well as a plural, as in *The doctor told me I've got a bacteria* or *That bacteria needs treatment*. This form is not used by most educated speakers, but if *bacterium* continues to be seen as a technical term, and avoided in everyday use, the situation may change. This is one of several problems caused by the irregular plurals of nouns of classical origin. (See also **criterion**, **data**, **dice**, **errata**, **media**, **stratum**.)

bad

As an adverb expressing 'manner of action', *bad* is normal after certain linking verbs, such as *look* or *sound*. *That sounds bad*, whether meant literally or figuratively, is the only acceptable form; people do not say **That sounds badly*. The majority of verbs in the language, however, prefer *badly*, with *bad* being used only in very informal speech: *She plays bad*; *I want it bad*. To some people, this informal adverbial use of *bad* is so unacceptable that they avoid the use of *bad* even after verbs where it is traditionally found in Standard English – preferring, for example, *He felt badly about it* to *He felt bad about it*. As a result, there is a great deal of inconsistency in current English. (See also **good**.)

barely

When this word begins a sentence, Standard English requires a following construction introduced by *when*: *Barely had I arrived when I was taken to meet Smithers*. You will sometimes hear *than* used in place of *when* in casual speech, but this use has never been given any status in the standard language. Similarly, the use of a negative word in the same construction would be considered incorrect (*I hadn't barely started*), on the grounds that *barely* already contains a negative element of meaning ('almost not'): the criticism of the 'double negative' construction in Standard English is long-established. (See also **hardly**, **not**, **scarcely**.)

Criticism is also sometimes made of *barely* as an intensifying word, when it is used in formal speech or writing. Constructions such as *barely ever*, *barely any* and (especially) *barely at all* are singled out, the claim being made that they involve an unnecessary degree of exaggeration. But the word is commonly used in this way in emphatic informal speech and writing, and many people are these days quite ready to accept it in more formal contexts.

bath

There are some interesting variations between the British and American uses of *bath* and *bathe*. In British English you usually *have a bath*; in American English you *take a bath*. (This difference is also found with certain other nouns, such as *walk* and *look*.) Both varieties use *bathe* in relation to going in the sea, and applying liquid in a soothing way; but only American English uses *bathe* for the domestic sense of taking a bath, and only the British *bath* a baby. *Bathtub* is commonly used in American English, where British usage prefers the noun *bath*. British usage also prefers *swimming bath* or *baths* for the public facility, though it also allows *swimming pool*; only the latter is used in American English.

Spelling is no guide to which verb is involved, in certain uses: *bathing* or *bathed* could be derived from either *to bath* or *to bathe*. In speech, however, a distinction is made: *bath* produces /'bɑːθɪŋ/ and /bɑːθt/; *bathe* produces /'beɪðɪŋ/ and /beɪðd/.

BC

See **AD**

be

As one of the most frequently-occurring verbs in the language, it is perhaps not surprising that the different forms of *be* have become the focus of usage questions. For example, there is variation over which form to use in *if*-clauses. The form *be* itself is infrequent in modern Standard English, and is restricted to very formal contexts: *If it be asked . . . .* The more usual construction, both in speech and writing, would be *is*: *If it is asked . . . .* However, you will still hear *be* in some rural regional dialects.

Within the verb phrase, the construction *been and* is a specifically British informal usage, expressing the notion of surprise: *He's been and got a new car!* This construction would be criticized if found in written English. The double use of *be* – *be being* or *been being* – has also attracted critical attention: usage manuals often call it awkward and inelegant. It should be noted, though, that there are cases where the sense cannot easily be expressed in any other way: it is important if you want to emphasize the duration of an action while using a passive voice construction: *Hilary's the one who ought to be being questioned about it.*

In the sense of 'because' or 'since', usage manuals do not consider *being* followed by *as*, *as how* or *that* acceptable in Standard English: *Being as you're tired, you might as well stay at home.* A construction with *as* or *because* would be the standard equivalent: *As you're tired . . .*
(See also **ain't**.)

because

All grammarians recommend care in using clauses introduced by *because*, in view of an ambiguity in the construction which needs to be resolved by the context. For example, the sentence *I didn't leave because I was cold* could mean either 'I didn't leave – the reason being that I was cold' or 'I did leave – but for some other reason'. Two points should be noted. Firstly, the ambiguity is only present when the main clause is in the negative: *I left because I was cold* is quite clear. Secondly, the ambiguity is often resolved in speech through the use of intonation: the pitch of the voice falls on the word *cold*, for the first interpretation, but gives it a 'lilting' falling-rising tune for the second interpretation.

There is a tendency to avoid the use of *because*-clauses as subjects of sentences, in formal writing: *Because you hate speeches is no reason why you should stay at home* illustrates a construction often heard in informal speech, but it is also criticized as inelegant and redundant, as the notion of 'cause' is expressed three times – *because, reason, why*).
(See also **reason**.)

behalf

Many US speakers (and formerly many British speakers) try to maintain a systematic distinction between the phrases *in behalf of* (or *in your behalf*, etc.) and *on behalf of* (or *on your behalf*, etc.), in terms of the direction of the activity involved. *In behalf of* is used in the sense 'for the benefit of'; *on behalf of* is used in the sense 'as an agent of'. According to this distinction, *I've come here on behalf of Mr Smith* means essentially 'I shall do what Mr Smith would do if he were here'; whereas *I've come here in behalf of Mr Smith* means 'I am here to further Mr Smith's interests'. Today, most educated users do not make such a distinction, using *on behalf of* for both senses. A similar preference is found for the noun use: *on your behalf* is the preferred form, with *in your behalf* being unused, or restricted to formal contexts.

below

See **above**

besides

Besides Jane, three people resigned. Question: did Jane resign? If you take *besides* in the sense of 'in addition to', yes she did – four people resigned altogether – and this is the usual way in which the word is used. However, many people also use the word to mean 'except for', especially in negative or interrogative contexts: *Besides Jane, nobody agreed with the decision*. Both senses have been in use since the early Middle Ages, so the risk of ambiguity can't be serious, but usage manuals recommend people to take care. The possibility of ambiguity is more real when people replace *besides* by *beside*, as is sometimes heard in casual speech. Standard English makes a clear distinction between *Besides her case, there were several boxes* and *Beside her case, there were several boxes*, where the preposition means 'next to'.

best

It is often maintained that *best* has an absolute sense – that only one thing can be 'best'. People who think this then have difficulty when they encounter such sentences as *These are the three best entries in the competition* (or, rather less commonly, *the best three entries*). The 'plural' use of the word, however, is attested from the earliest times: *They were the best of men* . . . .

Rather more widespread is the view that *best* should be carefully distinguished from *better*, on the grounds that *better* should be restricted to a comparison between two entities, and *best* to more than two: *That's the better essay* would imply that only two essays were being compared, whereas *That's the best essay* would imply that at least three were being compared. In fact, *best* is often used in informal speech for both of these contexts. Following a game of chess the other day, the loser congratulated the winner by saying *You definitely played best*. The natural feel of this expression can be sensed if you compare it with *You definitely played better*, which is ambiguous ('You played better than me? You played better than you did in your previous games?'). Many people find *better* excessively formal and unnecessarily precise, and use it only when the need for careful expression is paramount. On the other hand, many others value the careful implication which always accompanies the use of *better*, and take pains to distinguish the two.

Sentences expressing a recommendation by using *best* in the verb phrase, such as *You'd best find out by asking Jim*, are common in American English but infrequent in British English. The *'d* form expands into *had* in both varieties, but *would* is also heard in American English. Another way of recommending is through the use of *better*: *I had better leave now*, generally shortened in informal speech to *I'd better* . . . . In very informal speech, the *'d* form can be dropped altogether: *You best find out* . . . and *I better* . . . .

better
See **best**

between
In common with other prepositions, *between* governs pronouns in the objective case: *me*, *him*, *her*, *us*, *them*. However, a long-standing usage problem exists over the first-person pronoun when it is the second element in a combination: should it be *between you and me* or *between you and I*?

The first of these is the standard, normal pattern, as is illustrated by the fact that the reverse order of pronouns can be used: *between me and you*. The second is a special case, which does not allow reversal (we cannot say **between I and you*), or substitution by a plural form (we cannot say **between you and we*). It therefore has to be seen as a kind of idiom, which has developed as an alternative usage by people who think the *me* form too informal to be acceptable in careful speech, or who imagine the *I* form to be the norm in educated usage. In fact, the *me* form remains the educated norm, and it is the *I* form which attracts the criticism of usage manuals, as it breaks the normal grammatical conventions of prepositional use.

The controversy has been with us for many decades, and as a consequence, people's intuitions on the matter are no longer clear. Many people these days do use the *I* form in careful speech, and the *me* form in casual speech and writing, without any self-consciousness. For others, the situation is less natural and consistent, *me* continuing to be the generally used form, with *I* emerging, often self-consciously, on special occasions.

Standard English uses *between . . . and*, and not . . . *or*, . . . *as against*, . . . *as opposed to*, and the like. However, when people have a particular emphasis in mind, they readily slip into one of these other constructions. For example, someone who says *I want you to choose between the large book or the small books* is blending two sentence patterns: 'choose X or Y' and 'choose between X and Y'. It's a natural enough thing to do in informal speech, but in formal writing such a blend would receive criticism.

Between also attracts criticism when it is used along with *each* or *every* followed by a singular noun, as in *Leave a space between each line*. The critics are bearing in mind the original meaning of *between*, where the notion of 'two' was primary. Instead, they

recommend either a plural (*between the lines*) or an expressed alternative (*between each line and the next*). However, the etymological issue is widely disregarded: the singular usage is commonly found in educated speech and writing, and criticism is just as often directed at the recommended alternatives (especially the latter, which many find verbose).
(See also **among**, **dilemma**.)

biannual

Similarities in spelling and pronunciation have led to confusion between this word and *biennial*. *Biannual*, which is attested from the 19th century, means 'occurring twice a year'; *biennial*, attested from some 200 years earlier, means 'occurring every two years'. There is a world of difference between a biannual and a biennial publication, for example. *Biannual*, as the more familiar construction, is the one which is now increasingly being used in both senses. Because the uncertainty over which form to use is so widespread, several alternative expressions have emerged, such as *twice yearly* and *half yearly*. (See also **bimonthly**.)

biennial
See **biannual**

billion

The older British use of this term has the sense 'a million million' (10^{12}). The American use has the sense 'a thousand million' (10^9), and it is this sense which is increasingly to be encountered in international English usage. As a consequence, the British situation is now extremely confused, with both British and American senses of the term often used in the media. For some years the trend has been towards adopting the American usage as a uniform practice, especially amongst scientists, economists and other specialists, but the older sense still has considerable support in Britain, and in English-speaking parts of the world traditionally influenced by Britain. To avoid ambiguity, specialists often avoid the use of the term (and also of *trillion* and other derivatives), preferring to state the numbers involved using superscripts, as above, or in such a form as '10 thousand million'.

bimonthly

If you know the general use of *bi-*, meaning 'occurring twice' (as in *bicycle* 'two wheels' and *bilingual* 'two languages'), *bimonthly* seems innocuous enough. However, since the early 19th century, the word has been used in two competing senses, with the *bi-* element in one sense referring to the time period greater than a month ('once in two months') and in the other case to the time period within a month ('twice a month'). The same problem arises with *biweekly*. Unlike *biannual*, there is no alternative special term to help clarify the meaning (cf. *biennial*). As a consequence, attempts to resolve the ambiguity are common, by coining such words as *semi-weekly* and *half-weekly*. (See also **biannual**.)

biweekly

See **bimonthly**

black

As a noun (referring to someone from a dark-skinned ethnic group) or as an adjective (referring to the behaviour or characteristics of such a group), *black* (sometimes *Black*) is nowadays the preferred form in Standard English. Terms such as *black consciousness* and *black English* are widespread, and are used by members of the black community themselves, though *African American* began to come into fashion in the early 1990s. Alternative labels, such as *negro*, *non-white* and *coloured*, are available in the language, but are often felt to be offensive or demeaning. They may also be used in a specialized way, as when *coloured* is used in South African English for people of mixed white and non-white background. Even *black* is not immune from criticism: in Britain, for example, it can give rise to problems when used with reference to the many immigrants from southern Asia.

At the present time, the social situation is too fluid, and attitudes are too emotional, for any confident linguistic generalization to be made, other than to recommend sensitivity to the expressed preferences of the people concerned. This sensitivity is now very common, and has led, for example, to the avoidance of formerly common idioms (such as *nigger in the woodpile*, *black sheep* and *be in someone's black books*). In the USA, this sensitivity has often been extended (in a way which has sometimes attracted ridicule) to avoiding the use of the word *black* under almost any circumstances – for example, avoiding the use of the term *blackboard* in schools.

blond

The meaning of this word is, in principle, applicable to people of either sex, and French (from which the word derives) allows the use of two forms – one for masculine contexts (*blond*), the other for feminine ones (*blonde*). In English, the word is used both as an adjective and noun, but is generally restricted to women, female attributes, and male or female young children. In its written form, the word is therefore usually spelled with an -*e* ending, as in *Look at that blonde!* On the much less frequent occasions when a male is referred to, the recommended spelling is *blond*. However, this kind of gender distinction is not a feature of English grammar, nor does it appear in the spoken language (where *blond* and *blonde* sound the same). Consequently, usage has generally become less consistent, and when used as an adjective, *blond(e)* will often be found referring to features of either sex. In writing, the spelling *blonde* is commonly used when referring to female features, and *blond* referring to male, but these usages can attract criticism from those who are aware of the French gender distinction.

The same factors affect the use of the pair *brunet/brunette*, though the applicability of this notion to males is rare in British English, other than in certain specialized contexts (such as anthropological description). The restriction is less noticeable these days in American English. Most people do not know the *brunet* form.

borrow
See **bring**

both

There are several casual uses of *both* which have attracted criticism. Because the 'core' meaning of *both* is 'two', the use of the word to refer to more than two entities or notions is generally felt to be unacceptable, as in *The plan was satisfactory in both its aims, content, and timing*. Similarly, any use with words which *repeat* the meaning of 'two' also attracts criticism, as in *both alike, both together, both equally bad*, and *both the man as well as the women*. Usage manuals would recommend the choice of one expression or the other (eg *both bad* or *equally bad*), though this recommendation thereby excludes the option of using repetition for emphasis.

There is also a concern to maintain grammatical parallelism in the construction following *both*. *Both for India and for China* is acceptable, because *for India* and *for China* are parallel prepositional phrases. Similarly, there is a parallelism in *for both India and China*, where two solitary nouns are linked. But *both for India and China* attracts criticism, because this construction links a prepositional phrase and a solitary noun, and the critics find this inelegant.

Both generally suggests two things together, whereas *each* suggests two things taken separately. Usage manuals try to maintain a strict distinction here, and recommend avoidance of such sentences as *There's an apple tree on both sides of the garden*, arguing that it would have to be a very big apple tree to do this! Such arguments ignore the force of context, which tends to resolve ambiguity in real-life situations. Nonetheless, many speakers remain suspicious of *both*, and would certainly consider *each* a preferable alternative in several of its uses, especially when used in isolation (*Each pointed to the other*, instead of *Both pointed to the other*) or with pronouns (*We each got a letter*, instead of *We both got a letter*).

A similar situation exists with such phrases as *both the men and the women*, where in theory we could be referring to just two men along with an indefinite number of women, or an indefinite number of men and of women. The potential ambiguity is usually (though not always) resolved by context. *Both their cars* is a further example of potential ambiguity: the phrase could mean 'the car of each person', 'the cars of each person' or 'the cars belonging to the two of them, jointly'. Similarly, *Both cars cost £25 000* could mean 'Each car cost £25 000' or 'The two cars together cost £25 000'. *Each (of the)* would not be ambiguous.

Lastly, a choice is available in the language between no less than three constructions using *both* (also found after *all*): *both books*, *both the books* and *both of the books*. The last of these is sometimes criticized as verbose, but it can be an important way of emphasizing the individuality of the two entities. With pronouns, only the *of* form is possible (*both of us*), with a preceding *the* found in informal speech: *the both of us*.
(See also **each, each other, either**.)

bring

Standard English distinguishes between *bring* and *take* in terms of the direction of movement with reference to the speaker. *Bring* is used when the movement is towards a place identified with the speaker (basically, 'come here with'): *Bring it to me*. *Take* is used when the movement is away from the place identified with the speaker (basically, 'go there with'): *Take it to Fred*. However, speech situations are not always so clear-cut, and in informal speech *bring* is quite often heard in the sense of 'take', especially when the speaker sees the importance of a situation from the listener's point of view: *I'll bring the children back to you by six*. Needless to say, usage manuals, which tend to see language in black-and-white terms, don't like this at all.

The *bring/take* distinction is not unique. Other directional pairs in English include *come/go* and *borrow/lend*, which also give rise to problems of usage: *I'll come with you tomorrow* is similar to *bring*; *I'll borrow you my book* is definitely nonstandard.

British

Nationality names are always matters of sensitivity, as anyone knows who has unthinkingly replaced *British* by *English* when talking to a Scot about the Scots. *British* is the term which avoids having to choose between *English*, *Welsh*, *Scottish* and *Irish*, and is the only option for immigrants who have become citizens of the UK. There is no generally accepted noun for British citizens: they are variously called *Britons* (especially by newspapers), *Britishers* (especially by Americans) and *Brits*, though this last is informal, and sometimes felt to be insulting. None of these forms are much liked, and the adjectival usage (*I'm British*) is much preferred, as a consequence. When referring to characteristic features, the form *Briticism* is sometimes criticized, on the grounds that it is an abnormal lexical construction, there being no root *Britic-* to act as a foundation. It is however the form in most general use, especially outside Britain, though other forms can also be found (such as *Britishism* and *Britannicism*).
(See also **Scot**.)

broadcast

The preferred form of the past tense and past participle for this verb is *broadcast*, not *broadcasted*. The participial use is well established, as in *It was broadcast last week* and *The company have broadcast the news*. The form *broadcasted* is rare in general use, and is never used in the special field of broadcasting. In the past tense, there is rather more variability, but *broadcast* remains the preferred and specialist term. All of this constitutes an unusual development in the recent history of English, as most new verbs follow the general pattern of adding *-ed* to form their past tense. When the verb first appeared in the context of radio, in the 1920s, both variants were used, but presumably the influence of the root verb *cast*, itself irregular, caused the irregular variant to become the dominant usage. The point was much debated at the time by the broadcasters themselves.

burn

The past tense of this verb varies between *burned* and *burnt*, and it isn't easy to sense the difference between them. Some people seem to use them interchangeably. However, certain general trends are apparent. *Burned* is the usual form in American English, but in British English it tends to be restricted to intransitive verb use (ie without an object), where the continuing nature of the activity is implied: *The house burned (for several hours)*. *Burnt* is used for transitive constructions (ie with an object), as in *I burnt the cakes*, and is found intransitively only when the completed nature of the activity is implied, as in *The house burnt down*. *Burnt* is always used for adjectival constructions, in both dialects: *burnt cakes*, *burnt offerings*. (Other verbs like *burn* include **lean, smell, spell**.)

but

Few words have received as much critical attention from usage pundits as *but*. Many of the comments are directed at what critics believe to be an unnecessary use of the word. In particular, *but* tends to be criticized if it is used with another word that already contains an 'adversative' meaning: examples are *but however*, *but still*, *but yet*, and *but nevertheless*. Formal usage would recommend omitting the *but* in such cases, though their frequency in informal speech suggests that these pairings have a valuable role to play in the expression of emphasis. Likewise, *but only*, *but merely* and *but just* are felt to contain redundancy. *They have but only a short time* would probably be criticized by stylists as containing an unnecessary *but*.

There are several other grammatical contexts where usage manuals have considered *but* to be inappropriate, especially in formal writing. For example, some authors recommend it should not be used along with the conjunction *that* (as in *There's no doubt but that she'll do it*), on the grounds that it is an unnecessary complication. Nor is it admired in correlative constructions with *not so much*, as in *I'm not so much going to deal with politics, but with economics*, where the replacement of *but* by the more formal *as* is recommended. Lastly, there is objection to its use following negative verbs (as in *It won't take but an hour*), on the grounds that the 'double negative' meaning is better avoided (for example, by saying *It will take but an hour*). (See further, **however**, **not**.)

The position of *but* in the sentence always attracts attention. Stylists do not like it as the opening word (compare the similar criticism in the entry on **and**), despite the fact that, as an expression of emphasis, it is extremely common in speech (*But that's marvellous!*), and is the usual marker of an interruption made to disagree (*But as you said before* ...). Critics also do not like the placement of this word, when it means 'only', away from the noun phrase it governs (as in *time but for a few words*, where *for but* would be recommended). (See also the criticism of 'misplaced' **only**.)

C

cafe

The use of this word without the accent is now widespread in informal written English, and is increasingly to be found in shop signs, advertisements, etc. In speech, the informal norm is nowadays /'kafɪ/, with /'kafeɪ/ restricted to careful use. British English has also developed the humorous usages of /kaf/, written informally as *caff*, and /keɪf/, a deliberate mispronunciation for effect, based on the usual sound of the *-afe* ending in English. The tendency to drop written accents has become common in recent years in printed English, as part of the typographic fashion to promote an 'uncluttered' appearance in a text (also shown by the reduced use of the apostrophe, and the omission of full stops in abbreviations).

can

In formal English, in statements, a clear distinction is maintained between *can* and *may*: the former refers to ability (*I can yodel*); the latter to permission (*You may leave*) or probability (*I may fall asleep*). In informal English, however, the use of *can* to refer to permission is widespread, despite the efforts of several generations of school-teachers and grammarians to eradicate it. Many people recall such dialogues as: *Pupil: Can I have some paper? Teacher: You can* (ie you have the ability to get some paper), *but you may not. Can* is in fact becoming more frequent, and is now heard even on relatively formal occasions. *May*, correspondingly, is becoming more restricted in its use, and usually implies a clear distinction in status between speaker and person referred to: *You may go; He may leave now*.

A similar situation obtains for questions: *Can I ...?* is often encountered where *May I ...?* would traditionally have been expected. In negative statements and questions, the situation is complicated by the existence of alternative forms – *mayn't* alongside *may not. Mayn't* is felt to be awkward, and tends to be avoided, but the uncontracted form *may not* is also quite cumbersome on occasion, especially in questions: *Why may I not buy that book?*. As a consequence, forms using *can* are increasingly replacing *may* at more formal stylistic levels: *Why can't I ...?*. But *may* continues to be available for the most formal situations, in all grammatical constructions. *Cannot*, incidentally, is written as one word; *may not* (and the other negative forms of auxiliary verbs) as two.

Objection is sometimes made to such sentences as *You can't help but laugh* on the grounds that the construction forms a double negative (see further, **not**). People who try to follow this rule would prefer to say *You can't help laughing*. However, the *not ... but* construction has been in use for over a century, and is now found in formal as well as informal contexts.

cannot
See **can**

case
Stylists have often criticized what they feel to be an unnecessary use of the word *case* in examples such as *Is it the case that Mary wants to leave?* and *In many cases you will find ....* They would prefer to have *Does Mary want to leave?* and *You will often find ....* The root of the criticism probably lies in the overuse of the word in times past, so that it has become something of a cliche. Defenders of the locution argue that it adds an extra degree of emphasis, which the context justifies.

CE
See **AD**

cello
Few people now use an apostrophe in front of this word, showing its original status as an abbreviation (for *violoncello*). *'Cello*, and also *'cellist*, are occasionally used, but even in formal and technical contexts this spelling is now widely felt to be old-fashioned or pedantic. The word is no longer thought of primarily as an abbreviation, and indeed (as with *bus*) many people are unclear about what the full form of the word should be.

centre
When this verb is used without an object, it is found in construction with several prepositions. *On* and *upon* are the most widely recognized forms (*The argument centres on what she meant*

by that phrase), with *in* and *at* (for institutions) occasionally used: *The movement is centred at Edinburgh.* Informal usage has also developed the construction *centre around/round* (less often *centre about*), but purists condemn this expression on the grounds that *centre* refers to a focal point, and thus cannot be 'around' or 'about'. Defenders of the usage point to the emergence of a potentially useful semantic distinction between *centre on* and *centre around*, the latter being less definite.

certain

The absolute meaning of this word ('definite, beyond all doubt') has led to usage manuals criticizing any construction in which *certain* is qualified by such items as *more*, *most*, *quite*, *fairly*, *very*, etc. However, such qualifying expressions are found in formal as well as informal styles, and would generally be considered part of the standard language. (See also **complete**, **equal**, **unique**.)

chairman

In recent years, *chairman*, and other words in which a person's sex is explicitly represented, have attracted the criticism of those concerned with the status of women's rights in society. It is argued that such suffixes as *-man* symbolize the biases of a male-dominated society, and should be supplemented or replaced by forms compatible with sexual equality. *Chairman* attracted especial criticism at the outset of this debate, because of the distinctive and influential social role of the activity involved. Early proposals to revive an alternative form, *chairwoman* (in use since the 17th century) met with little success; but the 'neutral' form, *chairperson*, came to be increasingly used, especially in American English. The succinct *chair* is also now widely used: *Will you be chair? Madam Chairman*, which is the traditional mode of address for a woman in the chair, is still employed in British English, but is extremely formal.

The extreme way in which some of the feminist proposals were made has provoked a reaction by many (women as well as men), who adopt one or other usage 'on principle', considering the alternatives jocular or pejorative. Conference organizers, for example, often find it very difficult to make a decision over which form to use in their printed programmes, knowing that whichever decision they make is likely to be noticed, and be the cause of humour or offence to some participants. It is too soon to say what the outcome will be, regarding this set of words, as the social forces which initiated these changes in use are still in the course of development. (See also **anyone, -ess, Ms**.)

chronic

The informal use of *chronic*, meaning 'very bad' or 'very painful' (as in *My headache's chronic today, The hotel was chronic*), is quite common, despite the criticism of purists who, with an eye to etymology, insist that the only legitimate senses are those connected with long duration (*chronos* meaning 'time' in Greek). The pejorative usage is attested since the 1890s.

classic

Classic and *classical* are sometimes interchangeable when used as adjectives: there is little to choose between them in such phrases as *classic design* and *classical design*. *Classical* is more common in senses pertaining to ancient Greek or Roman culture. *Classic* has a more general range of use, including the broad sense of 'highest rank': *a classic treatise*, would therefore be different from *a classical treatise*, in that there is no necessary reference to early historical times. *Classic* has also undergone considerable sense change in recent years, developing such meanings as 'typical' and 'appropriate', and it has widespread ironic use in informal speech: *That's classic!* As a result, it is less likely these days to be a substitute for *classical*, which has no informal use at present.

The distinction between *-ic* and *-ical* is found in dozens of cases in English, but it is not easy to generalize about usage preferences, as different factors are involved. (See also **comic, economic, electric**.)

colleague

This is an interesting example of a word which is changing its status in terms of social class. It was traditionally used to refer to fellow-members of the various professions (ecclesiastical, academic, medical, etc.), or to office-workers in business. In recent years, however, it has come to be used by other groups of workers, especially those involved in negotiations using the trade union system. This extension of the word has been criticized by those who feel that the term confers special social status when this is not warranted; moreover, many groups of workers do not like the 'upper-class' connotations which the term carries. But there is certainly less restriction on the use of this word these days than ever before.

collective noun
See **committee**

come
See **bring**

comic
Comic and *comical* are sometimes interchangeable, in the general sense of 'amusing' (*It was a very comic/comical situation*), but usually the implications of the words are different. *Comic* emphasizes the humorous character or quality of a person, object, event, etc. *Comical* emphasises those funny or ridiculous features which tend to provoke laughter. (For other words with these endings, see **-ic**.)

committee
People sometimes express uncertainty over the correct form of the verb to use when this word is subject of the sentence: should it be *The committee is …* or *The committee are …*? Standard English in fact allows both constructions, depending on the point of view expressed. The singular verb form is used when the committee is viewed as a unitary group; the plural, when it is viewed as a collection of individuals. *A new committee is to be formed* is therefore far more likely than the alternative, as is *The committee are spending ages making up their minds*.

This is one of a number of nouns which permit a 'collective' interpretation, in addition to their normal plural use (as in *Three new committees have been formed*). They are, accordingly, called **collective nouns**. A collective noun takes a singular form of the verb when it refers to the collection as a whole and a plural form of the verb when it refers to the members of the collection as separate person or things. Other examples include *The orchestra was playing* vs. *The orchestra have all gone home* and *Their headquarters is near Holyhead* vs. *Their headquarters consist of 12 dilapidated buildings*. Because point of view can vary from one part of a sentence to another, it is possible to find collective nouns treated as both singular and plural in the same construction, in informal speech: *The family is determined to press their claim*. This usage would be criticized if it appeared in formal contexts, which would require either *are ... their* or *is ... its*.

(See also **family**, **government**, **group**, **headquarters**, **majority**, **means**, **pair**, **series**.)

compare

In informal usage, *compare to* and *compare with* are used interchangeably, but in formal contexts they are often given different interpretations. In the sense 'represent as similar', *compare to* is usual: *They compared the scene to a battlefield.* In such comparisons, the similarities are often metaphorical rather than real; the things compared are of fundamentally unlike kinds, and a general likeness is intended, rather than a detailed accounting. In the sense 'examine in order to note similarities and differences', *compare with* is usual: *She compared the first edition of the book with the second.* Here, the things compared are of like kinds, and specific resemblances and differences are examined in detail. Usage manuals stress the importance of preserving this difference, but there is evidence of both particles being used interchangeably from as early as the 17th century, and the elimination of the contrast in informal speech suggests that it may be unnecessary.

complete

Because *complete* has an absolute meaning ('total', 'whole'), usage manuals do not like it to be accompanied by such qualifying words as *more*, *most*, *very* and *quite*. However, this kind of qualification is common when people wish to suggest comprehensiveness of scope or thoroughness of treatment, where degrees of completeness are felt to exist: *Her book is a more complete account of the situation than is Smith's.* Also, informal English often uses these qualifications for emphasis: *He's the most complete idiot I've ever seen.* (See also **certain**, **equal**, **unique**.)

The archaic spelling *compleat* is sometimes used in relation to hobbies or other personal activities, where a humorous effect is intended. The literary allusion is to Izaak Walton's *The Compleat Angler* (1653).

compose
See **comprise**

comprise

The existence of several verbs of closely related meaning usually causes problems of usage, especially if there are accompanying differences in their grammatical use. This is what has happened to *comprise*, which is similar in meaning (and partly in appearance) to *compose*, *constitute* and *consist*: *The country comprises / is composed of / constitutes / consists of three main areas.* In formal usage, *comprise* is restricted to sentences of the form 'the whole comprises the parts': *The country comprises three main areas.* It is not considered acceptable to reverse the construction (*Three main areas comprise the country*), or to use a passive form with *of* (*The country is comprised of three main areas*). Informally, however, all three constructions are used. The *comprised of* construction is particularly common, and may even be heard in relatively formal contexts.

A distinction between *comprise* and *include* needs to be observed, if ambiguity is to be avoided, as the former refers to the whole whereas the latter refers to only certain parts. In *The team includes a Welshman and an Irishman*, there are several others in the team. In *The team comprises a Welshman and an Irishman*, the team has two members only.

consensus

The phrase *consensus of opinion* is widely used in informal speech and writing, and is sometimes used in formal speech. But usage manuals, aware of the definition of *consensus* (which already contains the notion of 'opinion'), often recommend avoidance of the phrase, on the grounds that it contains a redundant element inappropriate to careful expression.

consider

When *consider* is followed by a direct object (*I consider him a poet*), it has the meaning 'regard as' or 'think to be'. When it is followed by *as* (*I consider him as a poet*), it means 'study' or 'examine'. *As* is occasionally heard in the first construction in informal speech (*They considered him as a threat to peace*), but usage manuals would condemn this pattern on the grounds of potential ambiguity.

consist

Formal English makes a distinction between *consist of* and *consist in* which is sometimes ignored in informal speech. *Consist of* means 'be made up of': *The mixture consists of cement and oil. Consist in*, invariably used in talking about abstract notions, means 'have a basis in': *Freedom consists in everyone having the opportunity to choose*. Confusion sometimes arises because some contexts permit both meanings, as in *The game consists in/of one person trying to find another . . . .* Also, there is a tendency for *of* to replace *in*, but not in formal language use. (See also **comprise**.)

constitute

See **comprise**

continent

In Standard British English, *the continent* refers to the mainland of Europe, without the British Isles. But when Europe is specified (*We're travelling in Europe this summer*), there is a difference between American and British usage. To Americans this sentence would not exclude a visit to Britain. To the British, this sentence must mean leaving Britain. Since joining the European Economic Community, British English usage has become more complicated, however, as the implications of the notion 'being a part of Europe' come to be followed through. 'England is now part of the Continent', said one newspaper headline at the time, which illustrates the nature of the difficulty.

contrast

As a verb, *contrast* is usually followed by *with*: *The situation in Essex contrasts with that in Kent*. Alternatively, there is a construction with *and*: *I think we should contrast the Essex and Kent situations*. As a noun, when a distinction is explicitly drawn, the usual preposition is *between*: *The contrast between Jane and Jemima is remarkable*. When the contrast is implicit, *with* (less often, *to*) is used: *The contrast with last year is dramatic*. The phrase *in contrast* is usually followed by *with*, but *to* is also used, especially when the notion of opposition is being stressed: *This is in stark contrast to the price rise in Germany*.

controversy

This word has continually attracted attention, because of the way in which its stress pattern has begun to change in British English in recent years. From an original pronunciation, still found throughout the USA, in which *con* carried the main stress, there has been a widespread change to a main stress on *trov*. The change is by no means universal, however, especially in formal speech, and is consciously resisted by many people, especially those with a conservative temperament, who try to preserve the older pronunciation. The older form is recommended by a recent BBC booklet on pronunciation guidance, for example.

The reasons for the change are unclear. One explanation suggests that it arises from the tendency in English to reduce a sequence of unstressed syllables, thus preserving a more regular stress-timed rhythm. *Con'troversy*, on this account, displays a more natural rhythmic balance than does '*controversy*, which has three unstressed syllables together. An alternative explanation is that the change came about when people in England stopped pronouncing the /r/ in the penultimate syllable -*vers*-, thus turning the consonant cluster -*rs*- into a single consonant -*s*-. This altered the internal pronunciation 'shape' of the word. It no longer resembled other words with a consonant cluster in this position, which all have the stress on the first syllable: examples include *difficulty*, *excellency* and *epilepsy*. Instead, it came to resemble the words with no cluster in this position, which all have the stress on the second syllable: examples include *apology*, *rhinoceros* and *facility*. Because most accents in the USA retain the -*rs*- pronunciation, the stress has stayed on the opening syllable in American English – and the same thing has happened in other accents where /r/ is pronounced after a vowel (such as in Scotland). In most English accents, therefore, the pronunciation of *controversy* isn't controversial. (See also **dispute**.)

criterion

This is one of the most famous examples of the uncertainty which can surround the use of a noun of classical origin. Knowledge of how plurals normally work in English has led to the form *criterions*, but *criteria* is the only plural recognized in Standard English. Being unusual in shape, however, this word is then itself often taken to be a singular, and a new plural formed: *criterias*.

There is no sign of either *criterions* or *criterias* making any impact on educated usage, but constructions such as *a criteria* or *the criteria is …* will sometimes be heard by people who, as the usage manuals might say, 'should know better'. Only *criteria* as a plural is free of criticism in formal writing. (See also **bacterium**, **data**, **errata**, **media**, **stratum**.)

D

dangling participle
See -ing

dare

This verb is used in two different kinds of construction. The more common use is as a main verb, where it has a third person singular form in the present tense and a past tense form, and is followed by an infinitive preceded by *to*: *I dare to do it*; *I dared to do it*; *Does she dare to do it?* Its other use is as an auxiliary verb, where it has no third person or past tense forms, and is followed by an infinitive without *to*: *Dare she do it?*; *She daren't do it*. As these examples illustrate, this second use is usual only in interrogative and negative sentences; it is also less commonly used in American than in British English.

There are only two verbs in the language which have this particular kind of 'double' status (the other being **need**), and it is presumably the coexistence of the two constructions which has led to several areas of uncertainty in usage. Blends of the two constructions will frequently be heard, the most common one being the use of the main verb *without* the infinitive-marker, *to*: *We didn't dare go*, especially common in American English. Adding the third person singular ending to the auxiliary verb is sometimes heard (*He dares go*), but unlike the preceding blend this has no status in Standard English.

data

The grammatical status of the word *data* has changed considerably in recent years. Originally, it was used solely as a plural form (singular *datum*), but it has increasingly come to be used as a singular, in such constructions as *the data is, this data* and *much data*. No new plural in *-s* has developed, however, which means that *data* has now both a mass-noun interpretation ('the body of data, seen as a whole') and a count-noun interpretation ('several specific items of data'). There is less criticism of the singular usage these days than there was a few decades ago, when usage manuals would single it out as a particularly bad grammatical error. In current English, it is frequently encountered in formal as well as informal written English, alongside the more careful plural usage. But the issue is by no means resolved. The earlier controversy has left many writers uncertain as to which form they should use: *data is* may give an impression of ignorance (of the correct classical plural form), whereas *data are* may give an impression of pedantry. The field of computer data processing has given the singular use of the word a considerable boost, and in American English it is now well established. Nonetheless, there continues to be some reluctance to extend the singular pattern totally: forms such as *a data* and *two data* are still avoided. Because of the muddle, some writers have gone so far as to admit to avoiding the use of the word whenever possible. (See also **bacterium**, **errata**, **media**, **stratum**.)

decimate

The first meaning of *decimate* in English followed the sense of the form in Latin (where *decimus* meant 'tenth'): 'to kill one tenth of'; but since the 17th century the word has come to be used in a way which expresses the other end of the scale: 'to kill most of'. However, the verb cannot be used in all circumstances as a synonym for *kill*. It would be most unusual to hear someone say *I decimated him* or use the verb in a specific numerical context *They decimated 50% of the enemy*. Despite nearly 400 years of the broader usage, it seems we do still have an intuition about the etymology. This is probably due to the continued criticism of purist commentators on the language, who wish to preserve the earlier meanings of words, and who have kept the issue in the forefront of educated users' minds through its regular inclusion in usage manuals. (See also **aggravate**, **anticipate**, **deprecate**.)

definite

Definite and *definitive* both apply to what is precisely defined or explicitly set forth. But *definitive* more often refers, in addition, to what is unalterably final, and is not therefore usually interchangeable with *definite*. *A definite decision* is firm and clear-cut and might come at any time and be provided by anyone. *A definitive decision*, by contrast, usually implies the conclusion of a process of decision-making ('less definite' decisions having previously been made), and suggests that the issues are complex or important, requiring the attention of an authority. A shop may *definitely* (but not *definitively*) agree to deliver some goods, for example. A group of politicians who make a *definitive* decision are likely to alter our lives more certainly than if their decision had been only *definite*.

A usage problem arises when people are confused by the similarities in form and meaning between these two words, and impose a fresh relationship on them. A common assumption is that *definitive* is only a stronger form of *definite*. Also, there is a trend to use *definite* and *definitely* as if they were no more than emphatic forms: *That's a definite disadvantage*. In answer to a question, the word may simply be equivalent to a strong 'yes': *Will they sell? Definitely*. This last use is found in all styles of speech, but it has attracted criticism when used in formal writing.

deny
See **refute**

deprecate
The scholarly character of this word, and its similarity in form and meaning to *depreciate*, has resulted in a long-standing confusion between the two, with the former often being used in the sense of the latter. *Deprecate* derives from the Latin word for 'pray', and means 'express disapproval of' or 'deplore': *He deprecated the use of force*. *Depreciate* derives from the Latin word for 'price', and means 'belittle' or 'lessen the value of': *She always depreciated my achievements*. However, examples such as *She deprecated my achievements*, and associated forms such as *deprecation* and *self-deprecatory*, are increasingly to be found in all styles; and although this change attracts a great deal of purist criticism, it does look as if an interesting semantic development is taking place which may well become established in due course. (See also **aggravate**, **anticipate**, **decimate**.)

depreciate
See **deprecate**

dice
The relationship between this word and its singular *die* (in the sense of 'a cube used in games of chance') is now totally obscure in everyday use. The singular form is found only in the idiom *The die is cast*. *Dice* has come to be used as the relevant noun in both singular and plural contexts: *The dice are on the table* (referring to more than one of the cubes), and more recently, *The dice*

different

is on the table (referring to a singular cube). Although *dice* as a singular (along with a plural form, *dices*) is attested from the 14th century, this use still attracts some criticism, especially in American English, from purist commentators anxious to preserve the original distinction. (In the technical sense of a device which presses a design onto something, *die* and *dies* continue to be used.) (See also **bacterium**, **data**, **media**.)

different

Usage manuals have spent a great deal of space worrying about the correct choice of particle to use following *different* and *differently* in such sentences as *This glass is different – that* and *She argues differently – John. From* is the traditional standard form, in both British and American English, especially when followed by a simple noun, pronoun, or noun phrase. It is also possible to use *from* when the construction is followed by a clause, but this can lead to wordy or awkward phrasing (*The point he is making is very different from that which he made last week*), and *than* is widely used instead, especially when the following clause is elliptical: *They are more different today than (they were) last week.*

The use of *than* as an alternative to *from* is particularly common in American English, where its use with a following noun phrase has been common (and repeatedly criticized) for over a century. The British alternative is the use of *to* – a usage which dates from the 16th century. Purists criticize *to* on the grounds that it contradicts the etymological meaning of the prefix *dis-* (which underlies the form *diff-*): *dis-* expresses separation, and therefore (they argue) is more appropriately followed by *from*, as in the verb *differ from*. On the other hand, there are always stronger pressures at work in a language than popular awareness of etymology, and *different to* is these days quite common, except in formal contexts. Presumably people have drawn a parallel with *similar to*, and other such constructions.

dilemma

The *di-* in *dilemma* indicates its original meaning: a choice has to be made between two equal alternatives, as in *Our dilemma is whether to go in June or July*. Other usages attract purist criticism. These include the use of the word with reference to more than two alternatives (*The dilemma was whether to go in June, July or August*) and with reference to no alternatives at all (*We're in a dilemma about what to do next week*). Both are current in informal styles. (See also **alternative**, **between**.)

dinner

In its sense of 'chief meal of the day', the use of this word is standard throughout English, but different social practices over when the meal is eaten have linguistic repercussions. If the meal is in the evening, which is the convention in all 'upper' and some 'lower' class settings, the mid-day meal is referred to as *lunch* (or, very formally, *luncheon*). If the meal is at mid-day, then the evening meal is referred to as *supper* or *tea* – though usage varies greatly here, depending on such factors as the type of food served and the time at which it is eaten.

disinterested

Usage manuals attempt to maintain a clear distinction between *disinterested* ('impartial', 'unbiased') and *uninterested* ('indifferent'): the former lacks self-interest, whereas the latter lacks any interest. A well-used example illustrates from a judge, who should be disinterested in a case, but not uninterested in it. The usage problem has arisen because of the widespread use of *dis-* meaning 'lack of' in modern English, which has promoted a strong tendency to use *disinterested* (and also *disinterest*) in the latter sense. The trend has attracted the strongest of criticism from those who feel that the language is thereby losing an important semantic distinction; and indeed there can be ambiguity, on occasion. However, arguments about preserving the 'original' senses of these two words are misplaced. In fact, the *Oxford English Dictionary* shows that the use of *disinterested* in the sense of 'uninterested' is *earlier* than its sense of 'impartial'; and conversely, the early use of *uninterested* was in the sense of 'impartial' (both recorded in the early 17th century).

dispute

Perhaps because of its freqency of use in the media, in the context of industrial negotiations, variations in the stress pattern of this word have attracted particular attention in Britain in recent years. The traditional pattern is to have the stress on the first syllable, in the case of the noun, but there is a great deal of inconsistency (for example, the phrase *in dis'pute* usually retains the stress on the second syllable, even in the speech of people who often say '*dispute*). The related forms '*disputant* and '*disputable* also have an unstressed middle syllable, which may have been a factor in motivating the change; but in recent years variations have developed in some of these forms also (for example, *dis-'putable* is now often heard, and *dis'putant* sometimes heard), the change being in the reverse direction to that noted for *dispute*. (See also **controversy**.)

dive

Irregular verb forms often cause usage problems, and over the centuries there have been many changes, especially in the past tense forms. *Dived* is the regular past tense form of this verb in all styles and dialects of English; but *dove* /dəʊv/ is also found in American English, attested there since the mid-19th century. It seems to be increasingly common in informal speech, but usage manuals recommend its avoidance in writing. (See also **burn**.)

do

This verb is sometimes used informally in ways that formal constructions would avoid. Usage manuals recommend that, in such sentences as *They said he would fall ill, and he did do*, *do* should be omitted, because it is unnecessary. A similar concern is felt where *do* refers back to a form of *be* used as a main verb, as in *She's been to see the exhibition, as I have done*. Here too, the manuals would recommend the omission of the *do* form. The use of *don't* for *doesn't* was common in informal educated speech in the 19th century, but is now nonstandard in both British and American English (though widespread in regional dialects). (For *do* with *have*, see **have**.)

The use of *done* to mean 'completely accomplished' is not well established in formal contexts: *The project will not be done until next year*. Many people feel it is a somewhat 'empty' verb, in this context, and prefer a more specific word, such as *completed*. The substitution is especially likely if the sentence is felt to be ambiguous, with *done* capable of being interpreted as simply 'carried on', and not necessarily implying completion.

double negative
See **barely, but, not**

doubt

The verb *doubt* and the adjective *doubtful* are used in construction with following clauses introduced by *whether*, *that* and *if*. In positive statements intended to convey real doubt or uncertainty, *whether* is the usual choice, especially in formal contexts: *I doubt whether he can run so quickly*; *I'm doubtful whether he can run so quickly*. *If* is also found, but is somewhat less formal in tone. The use of *that* in such contexts has been criticized as 'weak' in meaning, but it is quite widely used informally, and in negative or interrogative constructions it is generally accepted: *Do you doubt that he wrote the letter?*; *I don't doubt that she's resigned*. (See also **but**.)

dove (verb)

See **dive**

down

Down and *up* are frequently a source of uncertainty, in their adverbial use in the context of travelling: do we go *down* or *up* to London, for example? The problem arises out of several conflicting meanings of these words: (i) *down* meaning 'to the south', 'in a southerly direction' vs. *up* 'to the north'; (ii) *down* meaning 'towards a centre of activity' (not necessarily in the south); (iii) *up* meaning 'towards a centre of activity' (not necessarily in the north); and (iv) especially in British English, *down* meaning 'from a place of importance to a place of lesser importance' (London and the leading university towns being traditionally seen as more important in this respect), *up* being the reverse.

Usage is therefore much influenced by our unconscious views concerning the interest and importance of the place in question, as well as its geographical location in relation to where we are. Speakers from all parts of the country might say *I'm going up to London*, though only speakers who feel themselves to be clearly south of the city would avoid saying *I'm going down to London*. Someone from the south would talk about *going up to Liverpool*, unless there were some reason for seeing the visit as less significant (for example, if it were felt to be a routine visit). The range of psychological factors involved is evidently quite complex, and it is probably never going to be possible to make any simple statement governing usage in this area.

drink

Drank is the past tense form of this verb, and *drunk* is the past participle, in Standard English. Sentences such as *She drunk the juice* are common in some dialects, but would be viewed as nonstandard. The adjectival forms, *drunk* and *drunken*, have a largely complementary range of use: *drunk* is generally used after a verb (*He was drunk*), whereas *drunken* is generally used before a noun (*a drunken driver*). *Drunk* is sometimes heard before a noun (*a load of drunk fans came in*), but this usage is criticized in many manuals, and would generally be avoided in writing.

due

A long-standing controversy in English usage concerns the use of *due to*, especially when seen in contrast with *owing to*. The traditional view is that, as *due* is an adjective, it can be used only when nouns are being related to each other, either joined by a linking verb (*The problem was due to his temper*) or in an adjectival construction (*The answer, due to the delay, was useless*). Criticism has focused on the adverbial use of *due to*, where there is no first noun to relate to, as in *Due to the snow, we arrived late* or *We arrived late, due to the snow*. Purists, anxious to preserve the distinction between an adjectival and an adverbial construction, have for over a century attacked this usage as illiterate, recommending as alternatives *owing to*, *because of*, *on account of* or *through*. The adverbial use of *due to* has nonetheless been widely employed in informal speech and writing, and is increasingly to be encountered in formal contexts (as in *Due to circumstances beyond our control...*), though not without persisting criticism from usage commentators. I have never understood why this particular point of English grammar has raised such strong objections. Whatever the reasons, one consequence of the controversy has been to make people over-sensitive to the issue. Many now worry about the use of *due to* in *all* circumstances, and replace it by *owing to* when there is really no need: *The problem was owing to his temper*.

E

each

When *each* occurs in subject position in a sentence, whether on its own, or as part of a phrase, usage manuals recommend that related verbs or pronouns should be in the singular: *Each has a copy of the book*; *Each visitor wants a map*; *Each of the boys has a pet*. In informal usage, especially in speech, this last type of example is often found along with plural forms of the verb and pronoun, because of the plural noun's nearness to the verb: *Each of the boys have a pet*. Even without the plural noun, the 'multiple' meaning of *each* can be enough to motivate the use of this plural agreement (*Each have a pet*), but this is less common. Plural agreement is normal in all styles whenever *each* follows a plural subject (*The visitors each have a copy of the map*), but if there is a compound subject, the 'singular' aspect of the meaning of 'each' is enough to motivate the use of the singular form of the verb (*Janet and John each has a place in history*). Uncertainty about whether to use a singular or plural verb following compound subjects is found in all styles, with formal styles tending to prefer the plural: *Janet and John each have a place in history*.

Another reason for the development of plural agreement in recent years, especially in informal speech, stems from the conflict between the 'neutral' gender of *each* and the explicit male/female reference of accompanying singular pronouns, in sentences such as *Each visitor looked for his map*. The masculine pronoun is the traditional one to use when a neutral (or 'generic') meaning is intended, but this is sometimes ambiguous, and since the 1960s has been attracting feminist criticism. To spell out the alternative is grammatically possible, but often very awkward (*Each visitor looked for his or her map*), and this has motivated the use of the plural form (*Each visitor looked for their map*), which these days is often heard, even in formal contexts. In writing, many people avoid the dilemma by rephrasing the construction, such as by making the subject plural: *The visitors looked for their maps*.

(See also **both**, **each other**, **every**.)

each other

Usage manuals traditionally recommend that *each other* should refer to only two entities, *one another* to more than two. There is certainly a tendency for modern usage to follow this principle but the distinction is by no means rigidly observed, and examples such as the following may be found in all styles: *The three kings stared at each other*, *Husband and wife should confide in one another*. These examples do however bring out the reciprocal meaning of *each other*, and in contexts where there is no such meaning the use of *each other* regularly attracts criticism. For example in such a sentence as *The three cars in the funeral procession followed each other down the street*, purists would recommend the replacement of *each other* by *one another*, on the grounds that the meaning 'each car is following each other car' is either unintended or impossible. But real ambiguity rarely if ever exists, with the consequence that here too the distinction is not rigidly observed. (See also **both**.)

The possessive forms of these phrases are written *each other's* and *one another's*. It is not standard written English to put the apostrophe after the *s*, though this is possible when *other* is used possessively as a plural noun: *The others' interest amazed me*.

earlier

The phrase *earlier on* has attracted criticism on the grounds that the *on* is neither necessary nor compatible in meaning with *earlier* (which is 'backwards' in time, not 'onwards'). In formal usage, accordingly, you will usually find *earlier* used alone; but informally, *earlier on* is common, the usage presumably having arisen on analogy with *later on*.

easy

This word is used in Standard English as an adverb in only a few idiomatic or informal constructions, such as *easy come, easy go* and *take things easy*. The usual adverbial form is *easily*, as in *The keys moved easily*. *Easy* is widely used in place of *easily* in the colloquial speech of many social groups, reflecting a general modern tendency to replace adverbs by adjectives (*It came out easy* – compare *She dresses good*, *He ran quick*), but this usage is regarded as substandard.

eat

The past tense form *ate* is pronounced both as [et] and [eɪt] in British English, the former being the more common. In American English, however, [eɪt] is the standard form, with [et] being heard only in a few regional dialects, especially in the southern USA.

economic

Economical is used only in such contexts as 'saving' and 'not being wasteful': *They found an economical way to live. Economic* is used when the meaning relates to the field of economics: *The programme tonight deals with the country's economic growth. Economical* is not acceptable in these specialized contexts; but *economic* is sometimes found as an alternative to *economical* in the general sense of 'saving' – as in a recent advertisement where a vehicle was said to be *an economic way of life for the motorist.* (See **-ic** for other words with these endings.)

either

When *either* is the subject of a sentence, usage manuals recommend that it takes a singular verb, and the singular form of any pronoun: *Either is able to give his consent.* Informally, plural agreement is often heard (*Either are able to give their consent*), and this is especially likely whenever *either* is followed by *of* and a plural noun or pronoun, in negative or interrogative constructions: *Are either of them in the area?*; *Aren't either of the disks usable?* These days, also, many people prefer the plural pronoun, to avoid having to use a masculine form in a general sense, which would attract the criticism of those concerned with feminist issues.

Either is usually limited to constructions involving two entities: *Take either* implies a choice of two, as does *Either disk would work.* The use of *either* to refer to more than two entities is occasionally encountered, but it attracts strong criticism from usage manuals, which recommend the use of *any* (or *any one*) instead. A similar criticism is voiced with regard to the *either ... or* construction, which formal usage tends to restrict to two alternatives: *She said they would enter for either the long jump or the high jump.* Informal usage, however, often uses this construction for more than two alternatives (*...for either the long jump, the high jump or the hurdles*), and this may even be encountered in formal contexts.

The *either ... or* construction raises other usage questions. Usage manuals generally recommend that the two conjunctions introduce elements which are grammatically parallel to each other: *He either obeys or leaves*, or *Either he obeys or he leaves*, but not *He either obeys or he leaves*, which is sometimes heard informally. Also, when two subjects are linked which differ in number or person, the verb agrees with the element nearer to it: thus we find *Either he or I am to resign* and *Either you or he is to resign*, though again, the rule is not always strictly observed in informal speech.

(See also **both, neither, none**.)

elder/eldest

Elder and *eldest* refer only to persons; *older* and *oldest* apply also to things. There is also a difference in construction: *elder* is not followed by *than*, and neither *elder* nor *eldest* can be used without *the* when following a verb, as in *Mike is the elder* (compare *Mike is older*; *Mike is older than Min*). These days, *elder* and *eldest* are largely confined to references involving members of a given family or business establishment, indicating age or seniority: *the elder Smith*, *the elder partner*. There are also a few set phrases, such as *elder statesman*. With reference to one's own family, *elder* and *older* are generally interchangeable, with a preference for *elder* amongst older people; when the reference is to someone else's family, however, *older* is more commonly used. In a round of introductions, for example, A might introduce B to C as 'my elder brother'; but C would be likely to introduce B to D as 'A's older brother'.

electric

Electric is used of anything producing or powered by electricity: *electric motor*, *electric light*. *Electrical* is more loosely related to the physical power of electricity, and is mainly used to characterize general concepts associated with the subject, or the people and activities involved in its study: *electrical engineering*, *electrical design*. (See **-ic** for other words with these endings.)

else

The possessive forms of constructions using this word are written with the apostrophe before the *-s*: *anyone else's*. Such forms as *anyone's else* would be considered substandard. There is a particular problem with *who*. *Who else's*, whether used singly or in combination with a noun (*Who else's book is missing?*), is felt to be an awkward construction, and usage manuals recommend its avoidance. *Whose else* is often used instead. Many speakers find this a more careful construction, and prefer to use it in formal contexts; others feel it to be just as awkward, if not more so. Only rephrasing can solve this problem: *Who else has a book missing?* Constructions such as *whose else book ...* or *whose book else ...* are not generally accepted in Standard English.

enough

The use of *enough* in construction with *that* is quite common, especially in American English; but many people prefer to use a construction with *sufficient* in formal contexts – *He's sufficiently angry that anything might happen* rather than *He's angry enough that anything might happen*. The greater formality of *sufficient* is also noticeable whenever it is interchangeable with *enough*, as in *They have enough/sufficient money for the journey*.

enquiry

See **inquiry**

equal

Purist critics take the meaning of *equal* very seriously, and argue that it should not be used as part of any comparison. They therefore object to such sentences as *We need a more equal distribution of wealth*, where *equal* means 'more equitable' or 'more nearly equal'. *Most* is less often encountered, but it will be found (*That's the most equal division of opinion I have ever seen*), as will *very* (*The two sides are very equal now*). The use of other adverbials with *equal* partly motivates these uses (*almost equal* and *exactly equal*, in particular), and there is at least one famous quotation which can be used to embarrass the purist position – Orwell's *Some animals are more equal than others*.

errata

The technical level at which the word *erratum* tends to be used means that the speaker is generally aware of its Latin origin, and has learned the irregular plural form, *errata*. The use of singular agreement with *errata* (as in *The errata in the book has been corrected*) would generally be considered unacceptable, therefore. (See also **bacterium**, **data**, **media**, **stratum**.)

especial

See **special**

-ess

The use of this suffix is changing, following the emergence of fresh attitudes to feminine roles in society. Originally it acted simply as a female gender marker, and had no emotional overtones: a *poetess* was simply a female poet. These days, several *-ess* forms are considered pejorative, in varying degrees, and would be avoided by males and females alike in general speech. *Authoress*, *poetess*, *sculptress*, and several others are rapidly going out of fashion. Some words remain relatively unaffected, such as *waitress*, *actress*, *heiress*, *baroness* and *abbess*, but even these can become a focus of contention on occasion. In a job description, for example, the need for sexual equality of opportunity would demand a neutral description for the job traditionally performed by a *waitress*. (See also **chairman**, **Ms**.)

etc

This form is principally found in informal writing, or in special areas such as technical reporting or business correspondence. Usage manuals do not recommend it for formal writing in general, preferring such phrases as *and so forth*. The construction *and etc* is not acceptable in any of these styles. Also condemned is the use of more than one *etc* at a time: *There were several blots, errors, etc etc*. This is felt to be a bad habit which some writers get into, and totally unnecessary. By contrast, the practice is very common in informal speech, where unimportance of subject matter is commonly indicated by saying up to three instances in quick succession: *So they gave me a pen, paper, etc etc etc*.

Because the original meaning of the form is 'and other things' (Latin *et cetera*), purist critics insist that its use is restricted to a list of things. A list of events, on this view, should not be followed by *etc* (*I swam, ran, etc*), but this restriction is generally ignored. Objection is also made to the use of *etc* when the idea of incompleteness is already implicit in such preceding phrases as *for example* or *such as*: *There will be many dangers, such as flooding, gales, snow, etc*. This convention is widely respected in educated usage. Lastly, the use of *etc* after a list of personal names is also widely felt to be somewhat demeaning or insulting: *I spoke to Martha, Mary, Jane, etc*.

ever

This word can be used in combination with *who*, *which*, *where*, *what* and *how*, but differences in writing indicate two distinct meanings. When written as a single word, the locution expresses a general meaning: *wherever you go* ('to every place you go'); *whatever you do* ('any action you do'). When written as two words, *ever* acts as an emphatic form: *Where ever did you go?* ('Where on earth did you go?'). After the superlative form of an adjective, the word adds an intensifying meaning: *The biggest ever circus*. An intensifying force also results from combining *ever* with *so*: *ever so interesting* ('extremely interesting'). This construction is primarily used in British English, and in informal speech may be heard without an adjective following: *I enjoyed the film ever so*. This usage is less common in male than in female speech, and may also be heard as a stereotyped mock form: *Ta ever so!* (See also **forever, however, rarely, seldom**.)

every

This word is used with a singular verb, and if there are any associated pronouns, these too are singular: *Every person has to decide for himself*. The singular meaning of *every* is very clear, so there is rarely a problem over agreement with the verb; however, a dispute can arise over agreement with a pronoun later in the sentence, especially when the speaker wishes to avoid one of the sex-marked pronouns. *Every person knows what they have to do* may therefore be heard, alongside the more careful (but much more awkward) *Every person knows what he or she has to do*. (See also **anyone, each, I**.)

The phrase *each and every* is sometimes attacked in usage manuals as a redundant expression: for example, *each and every day* is felt to be equivalent to *each day* or *every day*. But the extra emphasis conveyed by this phrase seems sufficient to explain its continued use in all styles.

everyday

This is written as a single word only when it is used as an adjective, meaning 'ordinary' or 'routine', as in *an everyday happening*. The stress pattern is 'everyday. Elsewhere, in its sense of 'each day', it is written as two words: *I go there every day*. The stress pattern is usually 'every 'day.

everyone

Everyone and *everybody* agree with singular verbs and singular pronouns in formal style: *Everyone wants to look his best.* In informal contexts, and occasionally in formal contexts, a plural pronoun is used, especially where we wish to avoid the masculine implications of the use of *his*: *Everyone wants to look their best.* Using *his or her* in such examples is generally considered awkward. In questions, the plural pronoun is generally preferred: *Everyone left the room, didn't they?* (See also **anyone**, **every**.)

Everyone is written as a single word when it has the general, indefinite sense of 'the group as a whole'. In this context, it may refer only to persons, and is not followed by *of*. *Every one* refers to both persons and things, seen as a set of separate entities ('every single one'), and may be followed by *of*: *Every one of the books was torn.* As a single word, the first syllable carries the strong stress: *'everyone.* As two words, *one* also carries a strong stress: *'every 'one.*

everyplace

See **anyplace**

except

In the sense of 'excluding', *except* is the prepositional form in Standard English, though *excepting* is sometimes heard in informal speech: *We all fell ill except Jane* (compare *We all fell ill excepting Jane*). *Excepting* is used without criticism only when it is preceded by a negative word or *always*: *They were all ill – not excepting my mother-in-law*; *The committee were in favour – always excepting Smith, of course.*

excepting

See **except**

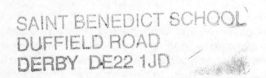

F

familiar

This word may be followed by either *to* or *with*. *Familiar to* has the sense of 'known to': *This town is familiar to me*. Things are familiar to people. *Familiar with* has the sense of 'good knowledge of': *I am familiar with his work*. People are familiar with things. Occasionally the contrast can be important: *You're very familiar to me* ('I think I know you') vs. *You're very familiar with me* ('You think you know me!').

family

Family may take a singular or a plural verb, depending on whether the noun is being viewed as a collective unit or as a set of individuals. In *The family has come into a fortune*, the speaker is thinking of the group as a whole receiving the money. In *The family are unable to agree about what to do*, the emphasis is on each member of the family holding a separate opinion. (For other nouns of this type, see **committee**.)

far

In statements, used alone as an adverb, *far* is felt to be extremely formal or literary: *We travelled far that day*. In questions or negative constructions, however, there is no such formal overtone: *Have you come far?*; *We haven't come far*. Similarly, the formal tone is absent when the word is preceded by *too* or *so*: *We've travelled too far*.

In the combinations *as far as* and *so far as*, formal English makes a clear distinction of use. *As far as* is used to refer to a movement in a particular direction: *I went as far as I could*; *We drove as far as Reading*. *So far as* is used to refer to the extent to which a particular situation obtains: *So far as I can tell, we're out of petrol*. However, the *as* form is increasingly being used in the latter sense.

farther, farthest
See **further, furthest**

fewer

Usage manuals take pains to distinguish between *fewer* and *less*. *Fewer* is the preferred word when reference is to numbers, or to entities considered as individuals, capable of being counted or listed. *Less* is preferred when the reference is to collective quantity or to something abstract. So, *fewer contributions*, *less pension* or *fewer opportunities*, *less opportunity*. In informal usage, there is a tendency for *less* to be used in place of *fewer*, especially when there is an implicit contrast with *more*: *No less than 30 cars were affected*; *There are 10 less computers in use now than there were last year*. However, even formal English will accept *less* when the contrast is explicit: *The company needs a few more results and a few less promises* (where *few fewer* would be unacceptable). *Less* is also standard in measurement phrases and after the word *number*: *The distance was less than 100 metres*; *I owed him less than £50*; *The number was less than I expected*.

first

In listing a set of points, there is some variation in usage over whether to use *first* or *firstly*. Usage manuals traditionally argue in favour of *first*, on the grounds that, because this word is used as an adverb (*I went first*) as well as an adjective (*the first prize*), the *-ly* ending is not needed. However, analogy with *secondly*, *thirdly*, and so on has led to the increasing use of *firstly*, even in formal contexts. As a result, usage guides have become more tolerant of three out of the four possibilities: *first ... second ... third ...*; *firstly ... secondly ... thirdly ...*; and *first ... secondly ... thirdly ...*. I have never come across anyone who recommends the fourth possibility: *firstly ... second ... third ...*.

First, *last*, and *next* usually precede a numeral in a collective expression such as *the first two chapters*, where the reference is to a single book. The reverse order, *the two first chapters*, is sometimes used with low numbers, but this construction can be ambiguous on occasion. It could mean the first chapters of two different books.

fish

There are two plural forms: *fish* and *fishes*. The former is the more widely used, referring to fish viewed collectively or as food: *The fish in the North Sea are no longer at risk*; *Those fish go well with white wine*. *Fishes* is used only when there is an emphasis on the individual fish in a group or an individual species: *The fishes come to the front of the tank when they're hungry* – and even here many people have a preference for the form *fish*, considering *fishes* to be colloquial.

Several other nouns have two plurals, including a number of animals (*We went looking for duck/ducks*), as well as certain technical notions (*formulae/formulas*). (See also **appendix**, **index**.)

flammable

Usage manuals are particularly worried about this word because of the real risks attached to its misinterpretation. The problem arises from the curious development which has led to *flammable* and *inflammable* both meaning 'highly combustible'. In this context, the prefix *in-* is an intensifier, and not an expression of negation: *inflammable* means 'able to be inflamed'. To say that something cannot be burned, we need to use *non-flammable* or *non-inflammable*. However, because of the widespread use of the prefix *in-* with a negative meaning (as in *invisible* and *inability*), it is very easy to misinterpret *inflammable* as if it were negative – and this would have potentially dangerous results. For this reason, *flammable* is the preferred term in technical writing and in contexts where people are being warned. In figurative usage, only *inflammable* is used: we talk of *an inflammable temperament*.

foot

With the emergence of metrical measurement, the usage controversies which have surrounded this word are likely to be of historical interest only, in the not too distant future. The problem arises only when *foot* is used as a unit of measurement, where it has alternative plural forms. In precise measurements, *feet* is formal, *foot* is informal: *six feet wide* vs. *six foot wide*. When *inches* is added, it is usual, even informally, to retain *feet*: *six feet two inches*, but *six foot two*. In compound adjectives *foot* is standard: *a six-foot ruler*. After the verb, usage reverts to *feet*: *The river was six feet wide*.

forever

In the literal sense of 'for eternity', formal British English prefers to write *for ever*, and to keep the words separate in longer idioms: *for ever and ever*. In the more everyday sense of 'constantly', it is usual to write a single word: *They're forever asking awkward questions*. Although the single-word spelling is attested from the 17th century, usage manuals generally recommend the earlier convention, of keeping the words apart. (See also **ever**.)

former

This word is used to refer only to the first of two entities in a list: *The speaker talked about buses and trains. The former, he said ...* When there are more than two entities, formal English disallows the use of *former*, preferring to use an alternative expression, such as *first, first-mentioned* or *first-named*. Stylists often recommend repetition of the name, to aid clarity: *The speaker talked about buses, trains and boats. The first of these, he said ...* or *The buses, he said ...* Some usage manuals don't support the use of *former* (and also of *latter*) under any circumstances, as in their view the backwards reference breaks up the smooth flow of the reading. (See also **latter**.)

-ful

These days it is normal to have a final *-s* as the plural of nouns ending in *-ful*: *bucketfuls, spoonfuls. Spoonsful*, and other such forms, is now felt to be somewhat old-fashioned or extremely careful.

further, furthest

In the general sense of 'additional', whether referring to time, quantity or manner, *further* has come to be the standard form: *further reasons, further notice, consider further*. It is also the normal form when standing alone, in the sense of 'furthermore'. *Farther* is only likely to be encountered in the sense of literal distance or direction: *The hotel is farther than we thought. Further* is encroaching even here, though, and is probably commoner in the expression of figurative distance (*Today the firm is further from a solution than ever before*), where *farther* is often felt to be somewhat old-fashioned. Change of usage has been slower in the case of the superlative forms, where *farthest* is still very common: *Who will travel farthest in that direction?*

G

gentleman

As a general reference, *man* is preferred to *gentleman*. The latter is used in special circumstances, and usually implies some kind of nuance: *He's not a gentleman* ('He does not act in a well-mannered way'), *That gentleman took my seat* (as might be said sarcastically by a lady). The form is widely used in direct address: *Ladies and gentlemen, I put it to you, gentlemen* ... It is also preferred when referring to a man in his presence: *Please ask this gentleman to wait in the corridor*, where *man* would sound quite abrupt. (See also **lady**.)

gerund

See **-ing**

get

When school-children use this word in their writing, they quickly find that adults don't much like it. It is said to be an 'empty' verb, with no particular meaning, which is prone to overuse. Teachers try to get the children to replace it with a verb which has a more specific meaning, such as *buy* in *I went to get a new car from the shop*. Usage manuals make the same criticism of adult uses of the verb, in any of its forms, in formal writing (even though it is sometimes the most natural and succinct form of expression available). (See also **lot, nice**.)

A particular recommendation is the replacement of *have got* by *have*, in both writing and speech. The *have got* form is certainly the norm for modern informal British English: *How much money have you got?*. The alternatives sound much more formal (*How much money do you have?*) and sometimes even archaic (*How much money have you?*). The *got* form sometimes allows a degree of emphasis which the *have* form lacks: *You've got to do it?*; *Have you got to go?*. In such cases, the notions of obligation and possession are reinforced.

Gotten is a common past participle form in American English, but it is not used when the senses involved are those of obligation or possession: *I've got to go*; *I've got three rabbits at home*. *I've gotten a new bike* means 'I have just obtained a new bike'. *I've gotten to do it* means 'I have succeeded in doing it', where British English would have to say *managed*, or the like. The use of *gotten* is not entirely based on distinctions of meaning, however: often, there is no obvious reason for its use, apart from speech rhythm and dialect background.

(See also **have**.)

go

See **bring**

good

Most speakers of Standard English try to maintain a clear distinction between the use of *good* and *well* following verbs. *Good* is the normal form after such linking verbs as *be, feel, seem* and *taste*: *That tastes good*; *It's looking good*. *Well* is the normal form with other verbs: *She swims/acts well*. When *good* is used with these verbs, as often happens in colloquial speech, especially in American English, it is often criticized as substandard: *She swims good*; *We played real good today*. (See also **bad**, **slow**.)

got, gotten

See **get**

government

When this word occurs as the subject of a sentence, it takes a singular verb in American English: *The government is determined to go ahead*. This usage is also to be found in British English, when the government is viewed collectively (*The government is ready for a fight*), but a plural verb is also possible when the government are seen as a set of individuals: *The government are undecided about which course of action to follow*. (See also **committee** for other nouns of this type.)

group

This noun can be used with either a singular or a plural verb depending on the sense. A singular verb occurs when the persons or things are considered as a unity, or to be acting as a unity: *The group is determined to fight against injustice*. A plural verb occurs when the persons or things are considered as a set of individuals: *The group were divided in their sympathies*. (See also **committee** for other nouns of this type.)

H

half

This word takes a singular verb when it is used with a singular noun: *Half the loaf was on the table*. It takes a plural verb when it is used with a plural noun: *Half the loaves were on the table*. In some cases, it can be used either preceding or following the indefinite article: *half a dozen, a half dozen; half an hour, a half hour*. The double use of the article (*a half an hour*) is often heard in informal speech, but is not a standard form.

hang

The usual past tense and past participle form of this verb is *hung*: *We hung the picture on the wall*. In the context of capital punishment, *hanged* is preferred: *The prisoner was hanged at dawn*. Usage manuals generally consider the use of *hung* in such a context to be informal or substandard.

hardly

This word is not used with a negative word in Standard English: *I could hardly hear what she said*. Constructions such as *I couldn't hardly hear* or *without hardly hearing* are often heard in colloquial speech, but are not acceptable in formal speech or writing. Following clauses are introduced by *when* or *before*: *He had hardly left when the fire broke out*. The use of *than* or *until* in such constructions has no status in Standard English. (See also **barely**, **not**.)

have

There are several differences between British and American English in the use of this verb. British English tends to use *have* alone to express the notion of a continuous state of possessing: *I have three brothers*. *Have got* expresses the notion of possession at a particular time: *I've got a sore throat*. American English uses *have* for both these senses. In negative constructions, British English prefers *have* alone, whereas American English prefers a construction using *do*: *I haven't any coffee* vs. *I don't have any coffee*. Similarly in question forms, British usage manuals recommend *Have you ...* rather than *Do you have ...* , and in responses *Yes, I have* rather than *Yes, I do*. However, the influence of American English is now very strong, and the *do* form is increasingly to be heard in all contexts. (See also **do**, **get**, **must**, **should**.)

he

See **I**

headquarters

People are often uncertain about whether to use this noun with a singular or a plural verb. The answer is that both constructions are possible, depending on the interpretation given to the noun. With a singular verb, *headquarters* is viewed as a single, unified entity, such as a point on a map: *The headquarters is three miles west of Granby*. With a plural verb, it is viewed as a collection of individual buildings: *The headquarters are little more than a group of old huts*. (See also **committee** for other nouns of this type.)

her

See **I**

here

Here, in the sense of 'in this place', is used after the noun when the construction is introduced by *this* or *these*: *this book here*; *these people here*. Constructions which place the word before the noun are very colloquial, and usage manuals recommend their avoidance: *this here book*; *these here people*. Similarly, there is criticism if a plural verb is not used when a plural noun follows: *Here are the answers*. However, the use of a singular verb is widespread in informal speech: *Here's the answers*. (See also **there**.)

him

See **I**

historic

Historic and *historical* have similar meanings, but they are rarely interchangeable. *Historic* largely refers to what is important in history, or to what has a long history attached to it: *a historic voyage*, *a historic city*. *Historical* refers more broadly to what is concerned with history or has an actual existence in history: *a historical account*, *a historical pageant*. A *historic novel* is an extremely important one, which may or may not be concerned with history; a *historical novel*, on the other hand, must be concerned with the events of history, but it may or may not have any importance. (See **-ic** for other words with these endings.)

home

British and American English differ somewhat in their use of this word. In the sense of 'in the house', British English prefers *at home* in such sentences as *Is Mary at home?* and *I stayed at home*. American English, especially informally, prefers *Is Mary home?* and *I stayed home*. *Home* also has a wider use in American English, corresponding to the British English use of *house*. For example, in selling houses, or in remarking about the quality of a house, American English would use *home*: *New homes for sale*; *They've bought a lovely home*. This usage is now increasingly to be found among British estate agents, but many people do not like it.

hopefully

In the sense 'let us hope' or 'it is to be hoped', this word is now very often heard, especially at the beginning of a sentence: *Hopefully the government will see sense*. It has however attracted a remarkable amount of criticism from purists, who want the word to be restricted to its literal sense as a modifier of verb meaning: *She said it hopefully* ('in a hopeful way'). They recommend, as an alternative, such constructions as *I hope that the government will see sense* or *I'm hopeful that the government will see sense*.

Why this particular word has attracted the critics' attention is not at all clear. There are many other words whose meaning varies in the same way, yet the critics have ignored them – compare, for example, *Naturally we'll go* and *We walked in naturally*. Defenders of the usage point out that it provides the language with a useful additional general meaning, in that the speaker does not have to say who is hoping. But I have never met an anti-*hopefully* person who has been impressed by this (or any other) defence.

house
See **home**

however

This is written as a single word, when the function of *ever* is to generalize or express contrast: *However we get there, it'll be late*; *She agreed, however, that she still loved him*. It is written as two words when the function of *ever* is to intensify: *How ever did you know that?* Here, the meaning is to express surprise or perplexity ('How on earth did you know that?'). Stylists also object to the use of *however* accompanied by *but* which, they argue, expresses the same idea twice: *But however, there were many who agreed*. (See also **but, ever.**)

I

I

Most of the personal pronouns display usage variations, especially in relation to the level of formality involved. The use of the subject forms (*I*, *he*, *she*, *we* and *they*) is traditionally preferred to the use of the object forms (*me*, *him*, *her*, *us* and *them*) in certain constructions in formal use. The best-known preference is for subject pronouns to be used following forms of the verb *to be* (*It is I*, *It was she*), though this usage these days is felt to be an extremely careful and artificial style, even in formal contexts. *It is me*, etc is now standard in all speech styles, unless there is a following construction (as in *It was he who told the vicar*), when formal speech requires the subject form of the pronoun, and informal speech the object form.

A similar situation obtains following *than* or *as* in comparative constructions, where formal writing prefers the use of subject forms (*Mary is bigger than I*), and other styles prefer the object forms (*Mary is bigger than me*). If the construction continues, the subject form must be used in Standard English (*Mary is bigger than I am*), though the object form is sometimes heard in some dialects (*She works harder than him do*).

The choice of an object vs. a possessive form of these pronouns is an issue when an *-ing* form of a verb follows. Purists insist on the possessive form, in such sentences as *I remember your doing that*, but these days the object form is the norm for informal usage. It is also often heard in more formal contexts (though the most formal levels retain the possessive form).

-ic, -ical
See **classic, economic, electric, historic**

if

Both *if* and *whether* may be used to introduce an indirect question, but there is a tendency for *whether* to be used in more formal contexts. In particular, it is more likely whenever more than one condition is being expressed and linked by *or*: *I asked whether the train would arrive on time or whether it would be late*. It is also sometimes necessary to use *whether* in order to avoid an ambiguity found with *if*. *Tell me if you want an answer*, for example, could mean either 'You are to tell me, if you want me to provide you with an answer', or 'If you do not want an answer, then do not bother to tell me'. Using *whether* in this sentence allows only the first of these possibilities.

ill

The word *ill* is often used as a polite equivalent of *sick*, especially in British English, where the connotation may be one of vomiting. Traditionally, it is used after a verb (*He is ill*) and not before a noun, where *sick* is normal (*sick child*, *sick pay*). However, *ill* is these days increasingly common before a noun, especially when the severity of the condition is implied: *We have a very ill child at home*. *Seriously ill* is standard: *seriously sick* could only be jocular.

imply

Standard English makes a clear distinction between *imply* (in its sense of 'hint') and *infer* (in its sense of 'deduce'). To *imply* is to state something directly. To *infer* is to draw a conclusion from what is stated. The distinction can be seen in the following sentences: *The inspector implied that there had been a crime* vs. *I infer from what the inspector said that there has been a crime*. The speaker/writer implies; the listener/reader infers. Usage manuals strongly criticize the use of *infer* in the sense of *imply*, which is quite often heard, even in educated speech. *Infer* is also more likely to be heard than *induce* (in its sense of 'infer by inductive reasoning'), which tends to be restricted to technical writing and discussion.

important

This word is often used as part of a connecting phrase, meaning 'what is especially significant': *More important, there are no trains on a Sunday*. In this context, there is a tendency, especially in formal American English, to add an *-ly* ending to the adjective, turning it into an adverb. Usage manuals generally object to this ending, arguing that, as the phrase is short for *What is more important*, the adjectival form should be retained. However, people seem to be paying more attention to the force of analogy with the many connecting adverbs ending in *-ly* (as in *Unfortunately, there are no trains on a Sunday*), for *importantly* is now common in current usage, and is increasingly to be heard even in formal settings.

inasmuch
See **insofar**

include
See **comprise**

index
Standard English makes a clear distinction between the alternative plurals of this word: *indices* is used only in the context of mathematical symbols and scientific signs in general; *indexes* is used only in the context of books and papers. Perhaps because of the academic settings in which these words are used, there is little sign of any confusion of use. (Compare the rather different situation with **appendix**.)

induce, infer
See **imply**

inflammable
See **flammable**

-ing
When a verb form ending in *-ing* is used as a noun, it raises different problems of usage than when it is used as a verb. The *-ing* form used as a noun (or **gerund**, as it is known in traditional grammer) is illustrated in *The inspector objected to my going*. In formal English, it is standard to use the possessive form of the item preceding the *-ing*-form, and this involves the use of the apostrophe in written English when that item is a noun: *She objected to Mary's going*. Informal English, on the other hand, often uses the neutral form: *She objected to me/Mary going*. And even in formal English, the use of the possessive is sometimes very awkward or impossible: *His absence prevented anything* (not *anything's*) *being accomplished*. Nor can it be used when there is an irregular plural noun: *We discussed the problem of mice* (not *mice's*) *damaging the wires*. In some cases, usage manuals recommend that the construction be rephrased: *His absence prevented the accomplishment of anything*. Similarly, in cases where the addition of an *'s* would lead to ambiguity, the construction

69

inquiry

is generally avoided: for example, in *He objected to his sons/son's leaving the room*, there would be no way of telling, in speech, which form was intended.

In formal English, the manuals also recommend that care is taken to avoid instances of the misrelated or 'dangling' participle – one which is wrongly attached to a noun or noun-like word, and which can produce an absurdity, especially if context is disregarded. A typical example is: *Lighting the fuse, the firework went off* (the firework did not light the fuse). In informal English, loosely related participial constructions are quite common, and do not usually give rise to ambiguity, because people sensibly take the context into account in arriving at an interpretation: for example, they know that fireworks do not light fuses, so the potential ambiguity does not arise. For similar reasons these constructions often pass unnoticed in formal varieties of English. But because ambiguity and incongruity do sometimes result from casual participle placement, and because of the strong purist desire to keep related constructions together, many people try to avoid the usage in contexts where their speech or writing is likely to be subject to close scrutiny. An alternative construction, such as *When I lit the fuse ...* would then be used. Incidentally, identical arguments apply to both the *-ing* participle (the so-called 'present participle') and the *-ed* participle (the so-called 'past participle'): *Cracked in several places, the vicar picked up the bottle*.
(See also I.)

inquiry

This noun, and the corresponding verb *inquire*, have variant forms in *enquiry* and *enquire*. The *in-* forms are universal in American English. In the UK, there is a tendency for the *en-* forms to be used in general contexts of seeking information, especially in the plural: *I'm making enquiries about a lost parrot*. The *in-* forms are more likely to be used in contexts of serious study or investigation: *There has been an inquiry into what caused the trouble*.

inside

When *inside* is a noun, it is followed by *of*: *I cleaned the inside of the car*. As a preposition, formal English prefers it to be used without *of*, in contexts of position or location: *I put the case inside the house*. Informal English sometimes adds the *of*, and this is especially common in contexts of time or distance: *We got there inside of an hour/a mile* ('in less time/distance than'). (See also **outside**.)

insofar

The writing of this form as a single word, followed by *as*, is now widespread, though it is still criticized by some usage manuals, which recommend that people should retain the earlier convention of writing separate words: *in so far as*. Exactly the same issue is raised by *inasmuch as* and *insomuch as*. The criticism is usually directed at *insofar*, where evidence of its use as a single form dates only from the 19th century. The other combined forms have a much longer history: *inasmuch* is regularly found from the 17th century, and *insomuch* from the 16th century.

insomuch

See **insofar**

-ise, -isation

See **-ize, -ization**

-ize, -ization

A few verbs ending in /aɪz/ are required to use the spelling *-ise*, in all written English dialects: these include *advise*, *disguise*, *exercise* and *surprise*. For the majority of verbs with this ending, though, American English uses the spelling *-ize*: *finalize*, *modernize*, and thousands more. The traditional British spelling is *-ise*, in such cases. However, British English is coming to be much influenced by American practices (as in this book), and now shows great variability, with some journals, newspapers and books using the *-s-* form and some using the *-z-* form. Verbs ending in *-yse* in British English (eg *analyse*) are also beginning to show signs of the American convention, which uses *-yze*. And there is evidence of change affecting some of the verbs which were formerly *-ise* only; for example, many dictionaries now give *comprise* an alternative spelling in *-ize*. The same trends in usage also apply to the derived nouns ending in *-isation*: *modernisation*, etc.

New verbs ending in *-ise/-ize* are often the butt of criticism by conservative language users, who feel that the excessive use of this ending is a source of imprecise thinking. However, the alternative way of expressing the notion 'to put into a specific condition' is often very awkward, and the economy of the one-word expression is very appealing: compare, for example, *publicize* and *give publicity to*. As a result, the popularity of this affix in modern English continues unabated, especially in technology: *containerize, miniaturize*. A few years ago, such coinages as *publicize* and *finalize* were attracting criticism. Today, other forms have moved into the firing line, such as *privatize, routinize* and *prioritize*.

J

join

Usage manuals often criticize the use of *together* after this verb, on the grounds that it is unnecessary: *I joined the pipes together*. The longer form does have a certain value in the expression of emphasis, however, and of course it is well-established in a few fixed phrases: *whom God hath joined together* ...

just

When expressing the meaning 'a moment ago', *just* is normally used with the present perfect form in British English: *I've just given the book back*. Informal American English allows the use of the past tense here (*I just gave the book back*), and this is now increasingly heard in informal British English. Usage manuals do not like this departure from a traditional 'rule', and disapprove of the use of these constructions in writing. The emphatic use of *just* also attracts criticism in written English: *It was just marvellous*.

K

kind

The constructions illustrated by *these kind of books are very enjoy-able* is widely used in informal speech and writing, and is well attested in formal styles (since the 16th century, in fact, including several uses by Shakespeare). What seems to have happened is that the plural sense of the noun phrase as a whole has led to the use of a plural instead of a singular verb. As the normal grammatical agreement rule has apparently been broken, this construction (and the corresponding construction using *sort of*) is perhaps best viewed as a kind of idiom. The abnormal grammer has been a traditional focus of criticism, though, and formal English thus tends not to use the construction, preferring to replace it by a consistently singular form (*this kind of books is ...*) or a consistently plural form (*these kinds of books are ...*), or to avoid the construction altogether (*books of this kind are ...*). Unfortunately, other problems surround the alternatives. Many people find them awkward and unidiomatic. In the case of the plural form, an alternative meaning is conveyed: *these kinds of* has the sense of 'the different classes of'. Similar problems affect interrogative constructions: *What kind of books are these?* is widely used, though some purists have argued that the construction should be *What kind of book are these?*

Other uses of *kind of* and *sort of* (often pronounced /ˈkaɪndə/ and /ˈsɔːtə/, respectively) are common in informal speech. In *I was kind of interested*, the locution means 'rather'. In *You sort of turn to the right ...*, it means 'more or less'.

know

In negative constructions, *know* may be followed by clauses introduced by *that*, *whether* or *if*. Any of these could be used in the following example, without attracting attention: *I don't know – the shop will be open*. The use of *as* in this construction is found only in informal speech, and usage manuals consider it to be substandard.

Particular criticism is made of the phrase *you know* when it is over-used in speech, on the grounds that it is a sign of lazy expression or unclear thinking. The problem comes to the fore in formal speech situations, such as television interviews, where we have a reasonable expectation that speakers will be clear and succinct, and where even one use of this phrase (or the others in this category, such as *you see* and *I mean*) can stand out. There are no grounds for banning this locution in all circumstances, however. In informal conversation, the situation is different. Here, *you know* acts as a convenient means of helping the dialogue along. It helps to signal the informality of the occasion, and provides speakers with a chance to change their mind and to think 'on their feet' (and listeners a chance to take in what is being said). *You know, you should apply for that job* is stylistically more intimate and less abrupt than *You should apply for that job*. And in *I sent back the book – you know, the book about gardening*, the phrase helps to signal to the listener that the speaker is engaged in the task of clarification. If we were all perfect speakers, who could plan the structure of each spoken sentence without hesitation, phrases such as *you know* would be as unnecessary as they are in writing (where there is always the opportunity to revise). Regrettably – and despite the best efforts of the usage manuals – this is not so.

L

lady

The changing use of this word has been a source of debate for over a century. Apart from its special use as a title within the British aristocracy, *lady* is the normal way of referring to a female person in her presence: *Give this lady a fresh cup of tea. Woman* would be rude, or imply some kind of nuance, in such a context. *Similarly, old lady* sounds far more polite than *old woman*, and to say of someone *She's a lady* implies a reference to standards of behaviour which are not found in *She's a woman*. In fixed phrases or special settings, however, *women* is a permissible variant for *lady*: we may refer to either the *ladies' finals* or the *women's finals* at a sport, or to a *young lady* or *young woman*. In such cases, *lady* is the form which implies an extra degree of courtesy or formality. On the other hand, in the context of jobs, *woman* is often used adjectivally without any special implication: *women students*. (See also **gentleman**.)

last

See **first**

latter

Latter is used when referring to the second of two previously-mentioned items: *We studied works from the 14th century and the 16th century. The latter were quite difficult.* It is sometimes loosely used to refer to the last-mentioned item in a sequence of three or more (*We travelled by car, train and boat. The latter ...*), but usage manuals are critical of this extension, and recommend the use of an alternative form, such as *the last-named*, *the last of these*, or simply *the last*. Similarly, *latter* is not acceptable when only one item is referred to: *Everyone looked at Jim. The latter smiled.* (See also **former**.)

lay

There is an unusual overlap between the forms of this verb and those of *lie*, and many people are unsure about which to use, as a result. *Lay* has the senses 'place, prepare'; its past tense is *laid* and its past participle *laid*. *Lie* has the senses 'recline, be situated': its past tense is *lay* and its past participle *lain*. The crucial difference in grammar is that *lay* normally takes a direct object, whereas *lie* normally doesn't. (In cases where *lie* does take an object, it is generally animate: *Lie the patient down on the table.* In this respect it contrasts with *lay*, which is used primarily with inanimates: *Lay the parcels down on the table.*)

The standard forms are thus as follow: *Fred laid the table* (not *lay*), *The hen has laid an egg* (not *lain*), and *The children lay down on the floor* (not *laid*). The alternate forms are sometimes heard in informal speech, and are common in some regional dialects, but only occasionally does the confusion surface in the written language – usually in idiomatic constructions, such as *to lie/lay low* and *the lie/lay of the land*.

lean, leap, learn

This cluster of three verbs displays a common feature: the use of alternative past forms, especially seen in British English – *leaned* vs. *leant*, *leaped* vs. *lept* (both pronounced /lept/), and *learned* vs. *learnt* (the former often pronounced /lɜ:nt/). In each case, the ending in *-ed* is standard in American English. The *-t* form is largely restricted to British English, but that dialect also uses the *-ed* form a great deal, perhaps partly under US influence. Where the two forms co-exist, there is a tendency for the *-ed* form to imply duration and the *-t* form to imply momentary action: compare *I learned to drive last year* and *Yesterday we learnt a new word*. *Learn* in the sense of 'teach, impart knowledge' (*I learned her to speak*) has no status in Standard English. (See also **burn, smell**.)

leave

In the sense of 'not interfere', *leave* is often interchangeable with *let*: *Leave the boy alone*; *Let the boy alone*. However, usage manuals often try to maintain a clear distinction between the verbs – *leave alone* for the sense 'leave someone in solitude', and *let alone* for 'not interfere with'. In the sense of 'allow', *let* is the usual form (*Let it go*), though *leave* is often to be heard in less formal speech.

lend

See **bring, loan**

less

See **fewer**

let

When a pronoun follows *let*, usage manuals recommend that it should be in its object form: *Let Mary and me start*. Some people consider the use of the subject form (*I*, etc.) to be preferable in compound constructions, especially in formal usage, because of the widespread 'feel' that these forms are more correct than their object counterparts (compare **between**): *Let they who disagree speak up now*. This is not a development which purists like very much. Nonetheless, there are some respectable precedents for it: *Let us go then, you and I ...* (T. S. Eliot).

Let us, in its full form, functions as a request to allow: *Let us go*. The contracted form cannot be used as a request, but only as a proposal for action which includes the speaker: *Let's go*. In negative constructions, *let's not* has widespread currency in both British and American speech. *Let us not* is formal everywhere. *Don't let's* is largely British English; *Let's don't* is occasionally used in American English.
(See also **leave**.)

lie

See **lay**

like

There is considerable antagonism to the use of *like* as a conjunction in formal spoken or written English. Instead, usage manuals recommend *as* (and also *as if* or *as though*). *Do like I told you* would become *Do as I told you*. Such sentences as *They act like they have money to burn* and *It looks like the car will be here at six* would have the *like* replaced by *as if*. The *like* forms are common in informal speech, however, and of course will be found in writing when it is a reflection of speech. Furthermore, when *like* introduces a clause in which the verb is not expressed, it proves to be generally acceptable: *The car looks like new*; *It looks like rain*; *It feels like wood*.

The restriction on *like* as a conjunction does not affect its other uses, though fear of misusing *like* often causes writers to replace it by a form with *as*. For example, usage manuals regularly object to such constructions as *Authors like Smith and Brown ...* , recommending *such as* instead. When the replacement is made thoughtlessly, however, it can result in problems. For example, the use of *as* could change the meaning, implying a contrast of manner or role, rather than a straight comparison: compare *She played the flute as a beginner* (ie she is a beginner) and *She played the flute like a beginner* (ie she plays as if she were a beginner). (See also **as**.)

literally

Usage manuals regularly insist that *literally* be taken literally. *The town centre is literally empty after 10 o'clock* is taken to mean 'No one at all is there'. They object to the use of the word simply as an intensifier, where it means 'in effect': *They literally went up the wall*; *There were literally millions in the cinema*. This usage is very common in informal speech, but would be condemned as a misuse of the word *literally* in formal settings.

loan

The use of *loan* as a verb is increasingly common, especially in American English, where it is encountered in formal as well as informal contexts: *I want you to loan me your keys*. The usage has been attested for centuries. However, many people, especially in British English, prefer to use *lend* as the verb in such sentences, restricting *loan* to its use as a noun: *I would like a loan of your keys*. But the influence of American English is strong, and such sentences as the following are now very common: *The government has loaned the painting to the British Museum for a year*.

lot

Teachers are prominent among those who find the use of *lot* empty and inelegant, when they encounter it in the written work of pupils: *a lot of money, the whole lot, lots of people*. The alternative is to use such phrases as *a variety of* and *a great deal*, or to introduce more specific terms (*Several thousand people were in the Square*), and these are widely preferred in formal speech and writing. (See also **get**, **nice**.)

lunch

See **dinner**

M

majority

This word is used only with reference to estimates of number, and not for general statements of quantity. We can say *The majority of people prefer to get up late*, but not *The majority of opinion is in favour of action*. In precise contexts, *majority* can apply to anything over 50%, but it is more commonly used to mean 'most' or 'almost all', where it is frequently preceded by an intensifier such as *vast* or *great*: *The vast majority of the population disagree*. Usage manuals recommend that the construction *greater majority* is used only with reference to a comparison of two specific numbers (ie two majorities), but loosely it is commonly heard as an equivalent to *great majority* (ie 'most of').

When *majority* signifies a specific number, it takes a singular verb: *The government majority was 128*. When it signifies the larger of two groups, it may be singular or plural, depending on the sense: *The majority is happy with the solution* stresses the unity of the group in question; *The majority are still arguing about what to do* stresses the individuality of the group's members. (See also **committee**.)

man

See **gentleman**

mathematics

When this word refers to 'the science of mathematics', it takes a singular verb: *Mathematics is an enormous field*. When it refers to 'the task of calculating', a more informal usage, it takes a plural verb: *Your mathematics are wrong*. The abbreviation in British English is *maths*, which likewise can be used with either a singular or a plural verb. In American English, the abbreviation is *math*, and this takes only a singular verb. (See also **acoustics, statistics**.)

may

May introduces a positive possibility: *You may have told me* means it is possible that you did. *Might* introduces a negative implication: *You might have told me* means either that I think you didn't, or that at best I am allowing it as a remote possibility. To use *may* where *might* is intended (or vice versa) can lead to confusion. For example, when I saw the newspaper headline *Drugs may have kept baby alive*, I thought the baby was still alive, whereas it transpired from the article that it was dead. *Might* would have better suited the intended sense. Usage manuals are therefore keen to point to the importance of the distinction. However, this shouldn't be over-stated, as in many cases no clear contrast of meaning is involved. *I may go to the beach tomorrow* and *I might go to the beach tomorrow* express little more than a difference in tentativeness. (See also **can**.)

me

See **I**

means

When this word has the sense of 'resources' (of money, property, etc.), it takes a plural verb: *Our means are sufficient to keep us going*. In the sense of 'way to an end', it takes either a singular or a plural verb, depending on the type of construction in which it occurs. Used with *a*, *any*, *each*, etc the verb is singular: *A means of transport is essential*. Used with *all*, *several*, *such*, etc the verb is plural: *Several means of transport are available*. Used with *the*, the verb may be singular or plural, depending on whether a collective sense of the noun is intended: *The means of transport is for you to decide* (collective meaning), vs. *The means of transport are extremely varied* (individualized meaning). (See also **committee**.)

media

When this word has the sense of 'means of mass communication', the standard practice is to use it as a plural noun derived from *medium*. However, the use of *media* as a singular is often heard (*Television is a lively media*), and a new plural form is sometimes used (*medias*), but neither of these forms have any standard status. The phrase *mass media* is more commonly encountered as a singular, and attracts less criticism. All of these uses must be distinguished from *medium* in the context of 'communication beyond the grave', where the plural is *mediums*. (See also **bacterium, data, errata, stratum**.)

meter
See **metre**

metre
In British English, the spelling *metre* is used for the senses of 'rhythm' and 'unit of length'. *Meter* is used for any of the instruments which measure (*gas meter*, *speedometer*, etc) and for the types of poetic line (*pentameter*, etc). American English uses the spelling *meter* in all senses.

might
See **may**

minimize
The original uses of this verb relate to an absolute value (to reduce to the smallest possible extent). Usage manuals therefore object when qualifications such as *greatly*, *somewhat* or *very much* are used with it. When a qualification needs to be made, an alternative verb, such as *reduce*, is preferred. But such constructions as *The gravity of the problem is somewhat minimized* are now heard in informal speech, and indicate a shift in the verb's meaning towards the more general sense of 'reduce' or 'lessen'.

Miss
See **Ms**

most
This word is often used as an alternative to the intensifier *very* (*It was a most amusing experience*), but usage manuals object to it, especially when it is used in writing, on the grounds that no explicit comparison is involved. Similarly, there is criticism of its use as an alternative to *almost*: *I think most everyone has gone now*. This is largely restricted to informal American English.

Ms
In recent decades, as a result of the changes in social attitudes towards the status of women, the two-fold classification of females into *Miss* and *Mrs* has come under attack. Unlike the

male *Master* vs. *Mr* distinction, the female contrast is not restricted in terms of age, but it does express marital status. The use of *Ms* has been advocated as an alternative, to be used for any woman who does not wish to be addressed as *Miss* or *Mrs*, for whatever reason. *Ms* has become increasingly adopted in written English, especially in letter-writing, where the writer does not know the married status of the addressee. However, the word's association with the feminist movement makes many (women as well as men) reluctant to use it. In speech, the word (pronounced /mɪz/) has so far had less success, and is often used in a self-conscious or jocular manner. (See also **chairman**, **-ess**.)

must

When *must* expresses obligation, it has a regular negative form: *I must ask her to dance* vs. *I mustn't ask her to dance*. In this sense, it is equivalent to *have to*, a form which is more common in this use in American than in British English. When *must* expresses necessity, it does not have a negative form: *I must get another bottle of milk* (where must = 'need to'). It is negated by using an alternative verb, such as *don't have to* or *needn't*. Similarly, when the looser meaning of probability is expressed (as in *You must be hungry*), there is no negative form; here, *can* has to be used: *You can't be hungry*. In this use, American English generally prefers a *have to* construction: *You have to be kidding* (compare British English *You must be kidding*). (See also **can**, **need**.)

myself

This word is often heard in informal speech as part of a compound subject or object, especially in some regional speech (Irish English, for example): *They asked Mary and myself to take the bus*. Usage manuals do not consider it a standard form, however, and in formal speech and in writing they recommend the basic form of the pronoun instead: *Mary and me*. (See also **yourself**.)

N

need

This word is used in two different constructions in Standard English. As a main verb, it takes an -*s* ending in the third person, is followed by an infinitive with *to*, and has a past tense: *She needs to buy a ticket*; *They needed to leave*. As an auxiliary verb, it has no ending or past tense, and takes an infinitive without *to*: *They need ask only once*, *She needn't leave until three*. The main verb construction is more frequent than the auxiliary use, which tends to be limited to negative and interrogative sentences. The auxiliary construction is more commonly used in British than in American English.

As always when two closely related constructions are available, there is some uncertainty of usage. Thus, alongside *No one need leave* and *No one needs to leave*, we sometimes hear *No one needs leave*; and alongside *Need we leave?* and *Do we need to leave?*, we may hear *Do we need leave?* British usage favours *We needn't* and *Need we?*; American usage favours *We don't need to* and *Do we need to?* It should also be noted that a sentence such as *We didn't need to leave* is strictly ambiguous: it could mean either 'and so we didn't leave', or 'but we did leave' – context being the only way of resolving the ambiguity in writing. (In speech, changing the intonation can help.)

(See also **dare**, **must**.)

neither

This word (as in the case of **either**) is restricted to a choice of two items, when referring to a preceding list: *The theatre and the circus have been mentioned, but Mark is going to neither*. If the list contains more than two items, *none* is the required form: *The theatre, the circus and the cinema have been mentioned, but Mark is going to none of them*. When the reference is forwards in the sentence, there is a strong tendency to restrict the list to two: *Mark is going to neither the theatre nor the circus*. A longer list may follow (*Mark is going to neither the theatre nor the circus nor the cinema*), but this is less likely in formal writing.

In formal usage, and quite often informally, *neither* takes a singular verb, even when it is accompanied by plural nouns or pronouns: *Neither book has been sold*; *Neither of them has been sold*; *Neither of the books has been sold*. The plural noun or pronoun preceding the verb nonetheless exercises a strong influence, and in informal speech and writing this can lead to the use of a plural verb: *Neither of the books have been sold*. The same influence is found in the use of the *neither ... nor* construction. When both elements are singular, the verb is in the singular: *Neither the book nor the letter has arrived*. When both are plural, the verb is in the plural: *Neither the books nor the letters have arrived*. And when one is singular and the other is plural, the verb agrees with the noun closest to it: *Neither the book nor the letters have arrived*; *Neither the books nor the letter has arrived*. However, purists do not like such 'messy' grammatical situations, and usually insist on the singular verb, even in a strongly plural context.

When the second element in a *neither ... nor* construction is a pronoun, the verb's agreement is with the pronoun: *Neither Jane nor I am going to the fair*. When both elements are pronouns, the agreement is with the one nearest the verb: *Neither she nor you are going to the fair*; *Neither you nor she is going to the fair*. When the alternatives follow a verb, there is a tendency in informal speech to allow *neither* to precede the verb: *They neither ate the cakes nor the biscuits*. The lack of stress on the verb makes ambiguity highly unlikely; but usage manuals nonetheless criticize this construction when it is found in writing, and in formal speech, on the grounds that *neither* should go next to the construction it introduces (compare **only**). Similarly, the replacement of *nor* by *or* in this construction, quite often heard in informal speech, attracts criticism on the grounds that there should be a consistently negative element throughout.
(See also **either**, **or**.)

never
See **seldom**

next
When this word has the meaning 'coming directly after, in time or sequence', it is usually not ambiguous. But when the anticipated event is very close, there is often uncertainty about whether the word is appropriate. For example, there is no ambiguity about referring to *next Friday*, if this is said on

Tuesday. But if it is said on a Thursday, a time reference of eight days hence would usually be intended; and if it is said on a Wednesday, there would often be uncertainty as to which of the two Fridays was in question. The use of *this Friday* as a way out of the problem (meaning 'the Friday of this week') is thus very common. (See also **first**.)

nice

This word has long been criticized by usage manuals as a 'lazy' word when it appears in writing. They argue that, instead of employing such a vague term of commendation, a more precise adjective should be used. Instead of *a nice picture*, perhaps, *a beautiful picture*; instead of *a nice computer*, *an impressive computer*. Stylists point out that there are invariably several specific terms which could be used in a given context, if the writer could be bothered to think them up. However, it is not solely a matter of 'bothering'. The reason that *nice* has come to be so useful is that it allows people to make a generally approving remark *without* having to be precise, and it has been used in this way for over 200 years. It is now widely used in informal speech situations. However, the concern for care and precision in formal writing makes it unlikely that it will become any more acceptable there. (See also **get**, **lot**.)

nobody

Nobody and *no one* take singular verbs and pronouns: *Nobody has yet gone home*; *No one knows the time of his appointment*. There's no difficulty involved in the verb agreement, but a problem arises over the use of the masculine pronoun for people who are sensitive to the need for equality of gender expression. *His or her* is avoided, because it is widely felt to be awkward. The only alternative is to adopt the plural form, which in fact was available in informal English long before the feminist debate developed: *Nobody knows the time of their appointment*. This form is normal in tag questions where no individual reference is involved: *Nobody's gone on the bus, have they?*. Because the use of a plural does not agree with the singular force of *nobody* and *no one*, however, the usage manuals tend to inveigh against it. (See also **anyone**, **people**.)

none

This word is one of the chief targets of purist usage criticism. It is found with either a singular or a plural verb, depending on the construction in which it is used. When it precedes or refers back to a singular noun, the verb is also in the singular: *None of the sand is wet*, *There's none left* (referring to, say, milk). A singular verb is also used when *none* can be interpreted as 'not one' or 'no one': *None of us was aware of the problem*. A plural verb is used when *none* is 'not any of a group of persons or things': *None have been more in need than the nurses*. Problems of usage arise when *none* can be interpreted as either singular or plural: *None of these cars is/are cheap*. Purists strongly insist on the singular form always being used in such contexts. However, people quite naturally tend to follow the sense, in these cases, and as long as the 'no single one' interpretation is not present, they would opt for the plural verb, in all styles. Only self-conscious awareness of the purist tradition would stop them. (See also **neither**.)

no one

When the meaning is 'no single person', two separate words are used: *No one of us is to blame*. When the meaning is equivalent to *nobody*, a hyphenated form is often used: *No-one is to blame*. This helps to avoid an ambiguity sometimes present in written English, where *No one is to blame* could mean 'The blame rests on everyone'. In speech, however, there is no ambiguity, as different stress patterns are involved: *'no-one* vs. *'no 'one*. (See also **nobody**.)

noplace

See **anyplace**

nor

This is the usual form in constructions begun with *neither*. When other negative forms are used early in a sentence, the continuation of the negative meaning requires *nor* if separate clauses are involved: *They have no experience of chemistry, nor does the subject interest them*. *Or* can be used when the constructions are dependent (*They have no experience or interest in chemistry*), but *nor* is also available as a more emphatic form of negation in such cases. The use of *and* with *nor* is common in informal British English speech (*Mike didn't go to the cinema, and nor did John*), but usage manuals find it unnecessary, and condemn it. Some also object to *nor* being used to open a sentence: *Nor did Jonathan much enjoy the day*. There are, however, many precedents in literature for this emphatically contrastive usage, and it is of course common in speech: *Nor me*. (See also **neither, or**.)

not

There are several constructions in English where two negative forms are used together in the same clause, and most of them have attracted the strongest criticism from manuals of usage. The most commonly used type, illustrated by *I never did nothing* (to mean 'I did nothing'), is widely used throughout dialects of English as an emphatic form. Speakers introduce the extra negative word to increase the force of the negation, as can be seen in the 'triple negative': *I didn't do nothing nowhere*. Constructions of this kind were part of educated speech and writing until the 17th century, but they are no longer acceptable in Standard English. Purists have taken the logical criterion of 'two negatives make a positive' and disregarded the semantic criterion (still used in many other languages) of 'two negatives make a more emphatic negative'. The purist explanation is widely quoted, but it is fallacious: if two negatives make a positive, then three negatives make a negative again, and on this count, *I didn't do nothing nowhere* should be acceptable!

Within Standard English, certain types of double negative are acceptable. There are cases where the negatives do indeed 'cancel out', as in *I can't not write* (meaning 'I must write') and *Not many books have no mistakes* (that is, 'Most books have some mistakes'). There are also cases of understatement (as in *She's a not implausible person*) and reinforcement (as in *They wouldn't leave, not even after the manager arrived*). And negatives are also sometimes correlated between main and subordinate clauses in certain types of sentence: *I shouldn't be surprised if he doesn't write*. (See also **barely, but, can, hardly**.)

number
See **amount**

O

O

This word is used for direct address, in prayer and invocation, in literary and religious contexts: *O God, O darkest night!* It is never followed by a punctuation mark, and it is always capitalized. *Oh* is used to express a reflective pause or a degree of emotion: *Oh, I see.* It is capitalized only when it is the first word in a sentence, and followed by a comma or (when the emphasis is strong) by an exclamation mark. There is some variation in use, with *O* replacing *Oh*, especially in American English.

odd

This word is used to express an indefinite amount in excess of a specified round number: *They must have 40 odd computers in the office*. It is not used with precise numbers (as in *42 odd computers*), and the hyphen should be used whenever there is a possible ambiguity: *60-odd people* vs. *60 odd people*.

of

The normal use of *of* after a noun is to express possession or close relationship: *the side of the house, a friend of my uncle*. The use of the 'apostrophe *s*' form is also available for these meanings when the first noun is animate (*my uncle's friend*), but this can't easily be done when it is inanimate: we do not say *the house's side*. In certain circumstances, it is also possible to use the 'apostrophe *s*' forms of the noun following the *of*: *a friend of my uncle's*. For this to happen, the noun in the *of*-phrase must be definite and animate: we do not say **a friend of a mother's*, nor **the side of the house's*. Also, the noun before the *of*-phrase is generally indefinite (*a friend* ...). You are unlikely to hear *the friend of my uncle's*, though in informal English the use of a demonstrative (eg *this, those*) is common: *I was talking to that friend of my uncle's*. The usefulness of the two constructions is that they can resolve an ambiguity which is often present when the 'apostrophe *s*' form is used. *Mary's photo* is ambiguous. *A photo of Mary* gives one meaning; *a photo of Mary's* gives the other. (See also **off**.)

off

This word is often followed by *of*, and sometimes by *from*, in informal conversation (*She got off of the bus*), but usage manuals strongly criticize this construction when it is found in formal speech or writing. It is nonetheless quite commonly used in educated American speech. Similarly, the use of *off* for *from*, in indicating the notion of 'source', is restricted to informal contexts: *He took the money off me* (or ... *off of me*). (See also **of**.)

Oh

See **O**

older, oldest

See **elder, eldest**

on

When expressing the idea of motion to a position, the prepositions *on* and *onto* are often interchangeable, but *onto* more strongly conveys movement towards the position, and often avoids an ambiguity present in *on*: *They jumped on/onto the boat* (where the use of *on* could mean either that they jumped onto the boat or that they were already jumping on the boat). In such contexts, *onto* is written as a single word. When *on* is a particle attached to another verb, however, it is written separately: *We're moving on to the next town*. The same distinction applies to *on* and *upon*: *They jumped upon the upturned boat*, *They caught up on their homework*.

one

Formal British English is strict about maintaining the use of *one* as a generalizing third person pronoun, and sequences such as *One should keep oneself warm, shouldn't one?* will be heard. American English is more likely to replace such sequences by forms of *he*: *One should ask himself* ... Usage manuals criticize any change of pronoun mid-sentence, especially if a change in number is involved: *One can do whatever they want*. *One* is particularly associated with extremely formal speakers, where it is often used as a replacement for the first person form even in relation to mundane topics (as in this often-quoted example, from a member of the British royal family a few years ago: *One fell off one's horse*, where the meaning is 'I fell off my horse'). Because of these associations, the usage is frequently the butt of satire, and these days is often avoided, even in formal speech.

When making a comparison involving the use of adjectives, there is a reluctance in formal English to use the word *one*: *Alan likes new cars as well as old cars* is preferred to *Alan likes new cars as well as old ones*. The use of *one* at the end of a sentence is considered to be stylistically weak (the word in this context cannot take a primary stress in speech). The reluctance is felt particularly when the noun is preceded only by a determiner: *Do you want to buy these books as well as those (books)?* is preferred to *Do you want to buy these books as well as those ones?*

In the construction *One in every ten books is returned to the library on time*, formal usage recommends that the verb should agree with the subject, *one*, and should therefore be in the singular. However, the proximity of the plural noun to the verb makes the use of a plural verb very common, and it is frequently encountered even in formal speech and writing: *This is one of the most embarrassing mistakes that have ever been seen in our office*.

one another
See **each other**

only
Most usage manuals insist that *only* is placed before the words it limits, in written English, to avoid what they see as a potential ambiguity: thus we should have *I saw only Fred* (and no one else) and not *I only saw Fred* (unless we are suggesting, for example, that 'I did not speak to him'). The tendency to place *only* away from the limited word, putting it earlier in the sentence, usually before the verb, is widespread in speech. It is rarely ambiguous there, because the stress pattern of the sentence indicates clearly which word goes with which: *I 'only saw 'Fred* (and no one else) vs. *I 'only 'saw Fred* (and didn't speak to him). Even in the written language, the context almost always makes it clear which is the intended meaning. However, the weight of grammatical tradition, alongside the risk of ambiguity, is enough to foster widespread observance of the adjacency rule in formal written English. There are enough genuine cases of ambiguity about to make the concern a real one: for example, I recently read that *The problem can only be clarified by asking the department manager*, and even after taking context into account I was left unsure whether the writer meant 'only clarify' or 'only the department manager'. (See also **neither**.)

Only, as a conjunction, is criticized in written usage in such constructions as: *They would have come, only the car broke down.* The use of *but* or some such phrase as *were it not for the fact that* is required in formal usage. (See also **but**.)

onto
See **on**

or

When all of the elements connected by *or* are singular, the verb they go with must be singular: *Coffee or tea is for sale at the interval*. When all of the elements are plural, the verb is also plural: *Either the cars or the bikes have to be cancelled*. When the elements are of different number, the verb generally agrees with the element closest to it: *Either the papers or the radio is wrong*, *Either the radio or the papers are wrong*. (See also **and, either, if, neither**.)

ought

As an auxiliary verb, *ought to* has no inflectional endings, and has the negative form *n't* or *not*: *You oughtn't/ought not to write*. It does not itself take an auxiliary verb, though in casual (and especially jocular) use such constructions as *You didn't ought to write* will be heard. An emphatic form, *did ought*, is also common in informal speech: *You did ought to write, you know*. In a sequence of auxiliary verbs, *ought to* is preferred in last place, next to the main verb: *We can and ought to do it*, and not *We ought to and can do it*.

In negative and question forms, *to* is often omitted, and these constructions are very strongly represented in regional dialects: *You oughtn't drive*; *You ought not drive*; *Ought you drive?* This also happens when the main verb is not present, being understood from the context: *Are you going to write to her? We ought (to)*. *Ought to* is often felt to be awkward in question forms, and *should* is used instead. In negative questions, there are three possibilities, ranging from informal (*Oughtn't she to write?*) through formal (*Ought she not to write?*) to very formal (*Ought not she to write?*). In tag questions, the *to* form is not used: *We ought to go, oughtn't we?*. Sometimes, a *had* form is used in the tag (though not without criticism from usage manuals): *I ought to go, hadn't I?*
(See also **dare, need**.)

outside

As a preposition, *outside* is sometimes followed by *of*, but usage manuals consider the use of the extra word unnecessary, and would not recommend it in formal writing: *Outside of the house, a crowd gathered.* The usage is somewhat more common in writing in American English. (See also **inside**.)

overly

This word is widely used as an intensifier in American English: *They have been overly critical about the book.* Although the usage is known from the early 19th century (and is found in Anglo-Saxon), it has attracted criticism as an unnecessary development, on the grounds that the same sense is already being expressed by the prefix *over-*, as in *over-critical*. It has had little impact on British English, apart from in Scotland.

owing to

See **due**

P

p

See **penny**

pair

This word can be followed by a verb in the singular or in the plural, depending on the intended meaning. The singular is used when *pair* emphasizes the unity of the components: *This pair of shoes needs mending*. The plural is used when the components are considered as individuals: *The pair are working together as a team*. When following a numeral (other than *one*), the plural is standard (*six pairs of shoes*), though the singular can be heard in informal speech and also in some technical contexts (*six pair of shoes*). (See also **committee**.)

participle

See **-ing**

penny

The change to decimal currency in 1971 had several linguistic consequences for British English. Chief amongst these was the question of how to pronounce the abbreviation *p*, as in *10p*. Immediately following decimalization, the pronunciation 'tenpence' was ambiguous, as it was unclear whether this would have meant ten 'old' as opposed to 'new' pence. (For a while, the forms *old pence* and *new pence* were used, but these have now largely died out, as people have become familiar with the new system.) The abbreviation *p* came to be used as an alternative, and it quickly became the dominant form. However, many people find the abbreviated form unpleasant, because of its phonetic association with the word *pee*, and prefer the form *pence*. It is certainly an unusual development, as English does not abbreviate other currencies – we do not say *10c* (for 'cents') or *10f* (for 'francs'), for instance. Contemporary usage is for *pence* (and *one penny*) to be used in formal styles, and *p* to be used informally.

people

This is the usual word for a group of human beings, considered collectively and indefinitely: *Several people came into the street.* *Persons* has a more restricted use: it can apply only to a specific and relatively small number, stressing the individuals involved: *This is a table for five persons.* Such examples are uncommon in British English (though not so in American English), where *person* tends to be restricted to certain fixed phrases, such as *person or persons unknown.* Some usage manuals insist on using *person* after numerals, reserving *people* for indefinite expressions only. In its singular form, they would also recommend that *person* takes a singular pronoun, traditionally *he*: *If a person has a vote, he should use it.* However, especially since the concern for gender equality in language, *they* has increased in frequency in informal speech. (See also **anyone**.)

per cent

Per cent and *percentage* are both used to express quantity with relation to a whole. The former is used in a specific context, always with a number: *75 per cent of the votes were in favour.* In informal writing, it is often written *percent*, and this is the normal spelling in American English, but usage varies between publishers. *Percentage* is never preceded by a number, and is generally qualified by a broad term indicating size: *A large percentage decided not to go to work.* It can also often be used loosely in the sense of 'small proportion' (*A percentage of the workers is still on strike*), but this departure from the earlier sense offends purists. If there is a verb following, its number is governed by the number of the noun used with *percentage*: thus we have *A large percentage of the people are ...*, but *A large percentage of the population is ...*

The symbol % is often used to replace *per cent*, especially as a space-saving device in contexts where several quantities are being expressed. It is not used in Standard English to replace *percentage*, though you may sometimes see it used in this way in very informal writing as a time-saving abbreviation.

percentage

See **per cent**

person

See **chairman, people**

politics

This word takes a singular verb when it is considered in a collective sense, as a science, art, or profession: *Politics is an interesting subject*. It takes a plural verb when it refers to the opinions, principles, or activities of individuals: *My politics are nothing to do with you*. (See also **acoustics, statistics**.)

practically

This word is now widely used in such senses as 'to all intents and purposes' (*The species is practically extinct*) and 'nearly' (*They had practically finished work when the snow started*), but these uses are often criticized by purists, on the grounds that, as the events in question have not taken place 'in practice', the word *practically* is inappropriate. Alternative words, such as *virtually* or *almost*, are recommended; but the extended usage is now encountered in all styles.

prefer

When the object of *prefer* is an infinitive, the subsequent construction is introduced by *rather than*: *I prefer to ride rather than to walk*. It is possible to omit the second *to* (*I prefer to ride rather than walk*), but usage manuals do not like the omission of *rather*. In all other constructions, *prefer* is followed by *to*: *I prefer whisky to gin*. *Than* is never used in such constructions, though *rather than* is sometimes heard in informal speech: *I prefer whisky rather than gin*. In such cases, the manuals – anxious to keep the two types of construction neatly apart – recommend the use of *to*, or an alternative using *have* (*I would rather have whisky than gin*) or *instead of* (*I would rather have whisky instead of gin*).

presently

The standard sense of this word is 'in a short time' or 'soon': *They'll be here presently*. However, a competing sense of 'now' is found in Scottish English, American English, and increasingly in other dialects of British English: *She is presently treasurer of the Association*. The usage has attracted fierce criticism from usage manuals, which argue that great ambiguity will be created if this development is permitted. Certainly, the possibility of ambiguity exists, but it is unlikely, as the accompanying tense forms tend to suggest one interpretation rather than the other: compare *They'll be going back home presently* (future) and *They're presently in the kitchen* (present tense).

programme

It is difficult to generalize about the spelling of this word in British English, because usage is changing. The American English spelling is *program* in all contexts. In Britain, the traditional spelling is *programme*. However, in the context of computing, the reduced spelling has come to be standard in British English, and it is beginning to emerge in other contexts, too, notably in the sense of 'schedule'. For example, in a recent edition of a journal for teachers, published in Britain, I saw several references to the *teaching program* to be used with a handicapped child, and a recent university report contained a reference to the *building program*. There is no sign of this spelling emerging in the more concrete senses of the word, however – such as with reference to radio and television shows or concert information booklets.

prove

Proved is the preferred past participle form of this verb in British English: *They have proved their point. Proven* is less often used, and tends to be found in formal (and especially legal) contexts. It is however the preferred form in American English. In all dialects it is the usual form to use adjectivally before a noun: *She has proven skills in running an office.*

Q

quite

Usage manuals often object to the 'weaker' senses of *quite*, where it means 'rather, somewhat': *The red hat is quite nice, but I'd prefer the blue one*. They argue that usage should be limited to the more positive senses of 'entirely, totally': *The two views are quite different*. However, the weaker sense is very widely used, especially in informal speech in Britain. As a result, there is always a risk of ambiguity between American English (where the 'strong' sense of *quite* is preferred) and British English (where the 'weak' sense is preferred). I recently had an argument with an American over the merit of a book: I said it was *quite good* (meaning that it wasn't marvellous, by any means), whereupon he took me to task for rating it so highly!

R

rarely

The use of *ever* following *rarely* is commonly used for emphasis in informal speech, but usage manuals consider it to be an unnecessary addition, and criticize its use in formal contexts. Generally acceptable are such combinations as *rarely if ever* and *rarely or never* (but not *rarely or ever*). (See also **ever**.)

rather

When pronouns follow *rather than*, they may occur either in their subject or their object form, depending on their role in relation to the rest of the sentence. For example, in the sentence *I told you rather than him*, *him* is used because it is governed by the verb *told*, whereas in *It was you, rather than he, who told the story*, *he* is used because it is part of the subject of the verb *cause*. In informal speech, there is a tendency for the object forms to be used everywhere, but this attracts the disapproval of purists, who try to maintain a strict subject/object distinction in pronouns whenever possible.

In constructions expressing preference, *rather* is generally preceded by *would*, either in full or abbreviated form (*'d*), when followed by a bare infinitive: *I would rather see him now than leave it until later*. *Should* is also possible in this construction. When followed by a clause, *rather* may also be preceded by *had*: *I had rather you saw him now*, and this is especially common in American English, where there is a preference for *had* also in statements using the infinitive construction. Of course, in informal speech, the distinction between *would* and *had* in statements disappears, as both reduce to *'d*. Nor is there a usage issue in relation to question forms, where *would* is the only possible construction: *Would you rather see him now?*
(See also **prefer**.)

reason

Usage manuals do not like the use of a *because* construction along with *reason*, on the grounds that such a construction would be expressing the same meaning twice: *The reason I left is because the pay was so bad*; *Because you left is no reason to complain now*. While these constructions are commonly used in informal speech, alternative constructions are recommended in formal speech and writing, such as using *that*: *The reason you left is that the pay was so bad*. A similar objection is made to *the reason why*, where the repetition of the notion of 'cause', which is also part of the sense of *why*, is felt to be unnecessary. Critics would prefer sentences to use *why* or *the reason* alone: *Why she did it was unclear*, *Her reason for doing it was unclear*. (See also **because**.)

refute

Perhaps because of its frequency in media debate and discussion in recent years, notably in negotiations between employers and trade unions, the confusion between *refute* and *deny* has attracted a great deal of attention. Standard English draws a clear distinction between them. Both verbs share the sense of disputing the truthfulness of a statement, but *deny* simply asserts that the statement is false, whereas *refute* stresses the marshalling of evidence in order to *prove* that the statement is false. Usage manuals consider the use of *refute* in the general sense of *deny* to be nonstandard: *The union refuted the suggestion that it had been obstructive*.

regard

This word enters into a wide range of constructions, some of which require an additional *-s* in Standard English and some of which do not. As a consequence, there is a great deal of uncertainty of usage. The standard constructions which don't use an *-s* ending are *to have regard to* ('to take into account'), *to have regard for* ('to show feeling for'), *with regard to* ('concerning') and *without regard to* ('without taking into account'). Those which do have an *-s* are *give regards to* ('greet') and *kind regards* (as a letter ending). In informal English, there is a strong tendency to use the *-s* form more widely. You will hear *with regards to*, in particular, though this attracts purist criticism, on the grounds that the constructions are grammatically different, and should be kept apart.

round

See **about**

S

same

When *same* is used as a pronoun, it is usually preceded by *the*: *Everyone got the same*. A more controversial usage is to use *same*, with or without the article, to replace another pronoun in the sense of 'previously mentioned thing or person': *Land is plentiful, but is there great demand for the same?* (where *it* would be preferred). The usage without the article is usually considered inappropriate outside of formal legal or commercial contexts (*I expect to receive same in a few days*), though even here it is rarely used nowadays. The elliptical omission of *the*, in such sentences as *He travels by bike, same as I do*, is a feature of informal English.

scarcely

Because *scarcely* has a negative meaning, usage manuals disapprove of its use with another negative word in the same clause: *They could scarcely hear her* is preferred to *They couldn't scarcely hear her*, and *They left with scarcely a sound*, rather than *They left without scarcely a sound*. Standard English also prefers the use of *when* rather than *than* with a following clause: *Scarcely had they left when the fire broke out*. *Before* is also sometimes used in such contexts. (See also **barely, not**.)

Scot

The people of Scotland are referred to as *Scotsmen* and *Scotswomen*, with *Scots* used as a more informal and neutral term. *The Scotch* is also quite widely used as a collective label. Of the corresponding adjectives, *Scottish* and *Scots* are the preferred forms in Scotland, though *Scotch* has come to be used in certain fixed expressions: *Scotch whisky, Scotch broth*. On the whole, *Scotch* is used when the adjective expresses a type of object, rather than its place of origin; *Scottish* is used when the sense of 'location in or relating to Scotland' is referred to: *Scottish universities, Scottish industries*. (See also **British**.)

second
See **first**

seem

Seem is a linking verb, and in Standard English is followed by an adjective: thus, *That seems good*, not *That seems well*. The construction *cannot/can't seem*, followed by an infinitive, is common in speech and informal writing: *I can't seem to move my leg*. Similarly, you will encounter the use of *won't*: *It won't seem to move*. These uses have attracted purist criticism, generally on the grounds that auxiliary verbs such as *can't* and *won't* relate to the main verb, and should not be made to apply to *seem*. Formal English would prefer alternative constructions, such as *do not seem able*, *seem to be unable* and *seems that it won't*. (See also **can**, **shall**.)

seldom

This word, as an adverb, may modify a verb (*I seldom leave town*), but does not follow the verb *to be* unless it is part of a further construction. Thus we have *It's seldom that Mary goes abroad*, but not *Mary's trips abroad are seldom*. It is also possible in a parenthetic construction, such as *When Mary goes abroad, which is seldom, she enjoys herself*. Usage manuals accept the idioms *seldom if ever* and *seldom or never*, but dislike *seldom or ever* or *seldom ever*, which are sometimes encountered in informal speech. The justification is that accompanying words should reinforce the meaning expressed by *seldom*, which is in the direction of 'never' rather than 'ever'. (See also **ever**.)

series

This word may be used either as a singular or as a plural noun. In the singular context, it refers to a single event, taken as a whole: *The present series is a failure*. In the plural context, it refers to a number of separate events: *Some TV series have been great successes*. When it has the singular sense of 'one occasion', *series* takes a singular verb, even when followed by *of* and a plural noun: *A new series of lectures has been planned*. (See also **committee**.)

shall

Usage manuals have insisted on a systematic distinction between the use of *shall* and *will* since the 18th century. It is recommended that *shall* should be used in the first person to express simple futurity (*I shall arrive tomorrow*), and in the second and third persons to express such meanings as obligation or determination: *Yes, you shall go to the ball*. *Will*, by contrast, is supposed to be used to express simple futurity in the second and third persons (*He will arrive tomorrow*), and such meanings as obligation or determination in the first person (*Yes, I will go to the ball*). The two verbs are thus thought to complement each other nicely. This suits the purist temperament very well, and the symmetry of the system, often reinforced by a punishing school discipline, has persuaded many people to try to write and speak according to these rules, especially in British English.

When we observe the way that the majority of people actually speak and write, however, we find that these rules are rarely followed – and it is questionable whether the language ever maintained such a systematic distinction. In any case, in modern English speech, contracted forms are in common use, where it is impossible to say which verb is involved (*I'll*, *You'll*, etc.). Also, the use of extra stress in speech, as a marker of emphasis, reduces any distinction between *shall* and *will* to little or nothing. American English has largely dropped any attempt to maintain the distinction, and uses *will* in all except the most formal styles; similarly, *won't* is standard usage for all persons, *shan't* being extremely rare. The distinction is more often maintained in British English, especially in formal styles and by older people in England (note, not in Ireland or Scotland). It is still in regular use there in first person question forms: *Shall I leave?*, *I'll leave, shall I?*.
(See also **should**.)

she

See **I**

shop

See **store**

should

Usage manuals argue that a distinction needs to be maintained between *should* and *would* parallel to that recommended for *shall* and *will*: *should* is to be used in first person forms for the expression of a simple condition, and *would* in the second and third person forms. The opposite situation obtains when other meanings (such as determination or compulsion) are to be expressed.

In practice, this distinction is hardly ever maintained. American English uses *would* with all three persons for expressing conditions, and prefers this form to *should*. British English usage is mixed: older people and more formal styles still maintain *should*, especially in the first person; younger people generally use *would*. Thus we have *If I had a ticket, I would go* (American English and some British English) and *If I had a ticket, I should go* (more formal British English). Similarly, with *like, prefer,* and related verbs, American English prefers *would*, British English formally prefers *should*: *I would/should like to go*.

In referring to past time, both the following constructions occur: *I would/should like to have gone*; *I would/should have liked to go*. There is no difference in meaning. The double use of *have* (*I would/should have liked to have gone*) is not a standard construction, though it will sometimes be heard in casual speech. *If I would have found it ...* is a possible construction in informal American English, but it is not used in British English, where a construction with *had* is standard: *If I had found it ...* Also, *would* is often used in a past habitual sense in American English (*Many years ago I would go swimming a lot*) where British English would use *used to*.
(See also **shall**.)

sick

See **ill**

since

See **ago**

slow

This word can be used as an adverb, as can *slowly*, but the two words are often not interchangeable. Usage manuals prefer the use of *slowly* in writing and in formal speech; but spoken commands and exhortations generally use *slow* (*Go slow round this corner!*) and it is the expected form in certain idiomatic phrases: *The clock is running slow*; *The trains are running slow today*. It is also the usual form with *how* (*How slow!*) and in some compound words (*slow-moving traffic*). An important point is that, if the adverb is used early on in a sentence, only *slowly* can be used: *We slowly skidded towards the wall*. (See also **bad**, **good**.)

smell

The past tense and participle forms of this verb may be *smelled* (the usual form in American English) or *smelt* (preferred in British English). The verb may be followed either by an adjective or an adverb, but different senses are involved. With an adjective, the sense is 'emit an odour': *The flowers smell beautiful today*, *That meat smells horrible*. With an adverb, the sense is 'emit an unpleasant odour': *The drains smell badly*. The latter sense is found when the verb is used on its own: *You smell!* (See also **burn**, **lean**, **spell**.)

so

So, used as an intensifying word, is quite common in speech (*I'm so glad that you could get here*), but some usage manuals disapprove of its use in writing, on the grounds that it is too colloquial and unnecessarily forceful. Used as a conjunction, the word is generally followed by *that* when it introduces a clause stating a purpose or reason (*Jane stayed up late so that she could see the eclipse*), but the *that* is often dropped in informal expression. In the expression of result or consequence, the use of *so* without *that* is more widely used (*The snow was very bad, so they stayed in the house*), though some stylists prefer alternative constructions (such as *and therefore they stayed in the house*). (See also **as**, **ever**, **far**.)

some

The use of this word as an adverb, in the sense of 'somewhat' or 'a bit', is common informally, but usage manuals strongly attack its use in formal contexts: *Things have improved some*; *It snowed some*. The informal use is common in American English. Also common (and increasingly in Britain) is the use of this word as an intensifier to mean 'marvellous' or 'remarkable': *That was some snowstorm!* (See also **any**.)

somebody

Somebody and *someone* take a singular verb, and, if a pronoun follows, usage manuals insist that this too should be singular: *Someone has left his newspaper on the chair*. Informally, especially in speech, plural pronouns are extremely common, but the verb always remains in the singular: *Someone has left their newspaper on the chair*. This places the usage critic in a dilemma. To support the former usage is to risk the antagonism of those who wish to see gender bias eliminated in the language. To support the latter usage is to break a traditional grammatical rule. Some manuals therefore argue for rephrasing (such as replacing *his* by *a*) or using a construction beginning with *There's a* .... Definite recommendations are premature. The changes in usage are taking place now, and it is too soon to be sure which pattern will eventually prevail, given the relative recency of the movement which has motivated the re-thinking of gender expression.

There is a stress contrast between *'someone* and *'some 'one* (where a person or thing has been singled out of a group): *Some one of us will have to leave on the first bus*. Also possible, though less likely (except in certain types of horror film), is a contrast between *somebody* and *some body*.
(See also **anyone**.)

someone
See **somebody**

someplace

This word, sometimes written *some place,* and used adverbially in the sense of 'somewhere', is standard in American English, with the spelling as a single word tending to be restricted to informal usage: *I left my bag someplace. Somewhere* is preferred in British English. *Some place*, in the sense of 'a particular place', is stylistically unrestricted: *I'll put it some place where you'll easily find it.* (See also **anyplace**.)

someway

Someway and *someways,* in the indefinite sense of 'in some way or other', are largely restricted to informal usage in American English and in some regional dialects elsewhere. *Somehow* is a more formal alternative. When written as two words, a more specific sense is expressed of 'some particular way or ways', and this is not stylistically restricted: compare *Someway we must do it* and *There must be some way that we can do it.* (See also **anyway**.)

sort
See **kind**

special
Special and *specially* are more commonly used than *especial* and *especially*, and some people maintain a difference in meaning between them. They use the *special* forms when the sense intended is 'particular, specific, as opposed to what is general or ordinary': *They have displayed a special concern about our situation*; *Many people have been specially trained for the job.* The *especial* forms are used when the sense is that of 'preeminence, exceptional degree': *Mary is an especially gifted member of that family*; *It's unusual, especially these days.* Purists advocate the distinction, but for a large number of people the two sets of words are interchangeable.

spell
Both *spelled* and *spelt* are used as past tenses and participles. The former is standard in American English; the latter is the usual form in British English. Several other verbs display this kind of distinction, such as *spill* and *spoil.* (See also **burn, lean, smell**.)

spill
See **spell**

split infinitive
See **to**

spoil
See **spell**

statistics
This word, like *mathematics*, is used with a singular verb when it refers to the academic subject: *Statistics is a complex field.* It is used with a plural verb when it refers to a particular collection of numerical data: *The statistics about pay rises aren't impressive.* A singular usage is also possible, and has been attested for well over a century: *That's an important statistic.* (See also **acoustics, mathematics**.)

still

Standard English requires the use of the present perfect verb form with *still*: *I have still got a bike*. American English permits the use of the simple past tense: *I still got a bike*. The latter usage will also be encountered nowadays in informal British speech.

Usage manuals dislike the use of *still* with a verb where the meaning of continuity is dominant, such as *continue* or *remain*, on the grounds that the same meaning is being unnecessarily repeated: *The riots are still continuing in the towns*. On the other hand, it could be argued that the repetition adds an extra note of emphasis or insistence.

store

This word is used in all varieties of English in the sense of 'warehouse'. When referring to a building where goods are sold, it is in general use in American English, where British English would traditionally use *shop*. *Store* has come to be used in British English in recent years, however, in the sense of a large shop containing many departments (*department store*), and also, on a smaller scale, for the relatively large, general-purpose shop found in villages and suburbs. *Shop* is used in all varieties of English in the sense of 'place where a certain type of work is done': *repair shop*, *barber('s) shop*. In American English, especially in recent years, *shop* has come to be used for a certain type of store, especially one which specializes in fashionable goods or activities, such as hairdressing or gifts. A mock-archaic spelling is often used in such settings: *Gift Shoppe*.

stratum

The standard plural form is *strata*: *All strata of society have been influenced by the price rises*. *Stratums* and *stratas* are both sometimes used by people who are unaware of the irregular status of this noun, but these forms are severely criticized by usage manuals. Likewise, the use of *strata* as a singular is not standard, though it is often heard: *One particular strata has attracted the attention of critics*. (See also **bacterium**, **data**, **errata**.)

such

Usage manuals recommend that, when *such* is introducing an example, it should be followed by *as*, rather than by a pronoun (*that, which*): *I shall investigate such cases of difficulty as have been reported*. However, the influence of the relative clause construction (*the difficulty which has been reported*) is very strong, and the alternative usages are common, both in speech and in writing. (See also **that**.)

Following *such as*, the manuals recommend the use of the subject form of a personal pronoun, and this is normal in formal English: *Writers such as he have always had a rough time*. Informal English usually uses the object form of the pronoun in such cases, and when the pronoun occurs at the end of a sentence this is quite common even in formal contexts: *I've never before come across a boy such as him*.
(See also **like**.)

sufficient
See **enough**

T

take

See **bring**

than

One of the most persistent questions about English usage is which pronoun to use after *than*. Usage manuals recommend that sentences such as *He is bigger than I* should be preferred to *He is bigger than me*, on the grounds that *than* is here functioning as a conjunction, not a preposition, and therefore the sentence is short for *He is bigger than I am*. Similarly, *They persuaded him more than her* is said to be short for *They persuaded him more than they persuaded her*. In informal usage, the object form of pronouns is generally used in all positions, and with third person forms this usage will often be encountered even in relatively formal contexts: *John is much taller than him*, where *John is much taller than he* is widely felt to be stilted.

When followed by a clause, the use of *what* is generally considered to be very informal, and many people avoid it altogether: *Mary is looking much happier today than (what) she was yesterday.* Usage manuals are usually horrified by it.
(See also **as**, **different**, **I**.)

that

When used as relative pronouns (that is, pronouns which introduce clauses), *that* and *which* are often interchangeable: *There's the car that/which had the accident. That* is the more widely used form, as it may refer to people, animals and things, whereas *which* cannot refer to people. On the other hand, usage manuals widely consider *that* to be less formal than *which*, and recommend the use of the latter in all possible contexts. There is nonetheless a tendency for *that* to be used when the clause is restrictive – that is, a clause which is an essential part of the identification of the preceding noun: *A law that is not supported by the public is a difficult law to enforce.* In such cases, there must be no commas surrounding the relative clause, and often the pronoun is dropped: *A law not supported by the public . . . . Which* is more likely to be used when the clause is nonrestrictive – that is, it provides information that is not essential to the definition of the preceding noun: *The latest law, which I read about yesterday, is unpopular*. In such cases, the clause is set off by commas, and the pronoun cannot be dropped. In sentences where *that* is used as a preceding pronoun, *which* is generally used, whether the clause is restrictive or not: *It is larger than that which you saw in the park*. Few writers would fail to feel the clash which comes from having two uses of *that* side by side.

In speech, the distinction between restrictive and nonrestrictive is usually signalled by intonation and pause (which correspond to the use of the comma in writing). *The typewriter which needs cleaning is on the table*, if said with pauses preceding and following the clause, means that there is only one typewriter; said without these pauses, it means that there is more than one (the other typewriter does not need cleaning). In fast speech, however, the distinction often disappears, and only context can resolve the ambiguity.

That, used as a conjunction, is often omitted in informal speech and writing, and sometimes in formal contexts, as long as there is no danger of ambiguity: *He said (that) he would return later*. An example of ambiguity occurs in sentences where *that* precedes a reference to time: *He said that on January 1st there would be an election* (where to omit *that* would permit the interpretation that the saying took place on January 1st).
(See also **so**, **this**, **what**.)

the
See **a**

them
See **I**

there
When this word is used before a linking verb, such as *be* or *seem*, the verb agrees in number with the following noun: *There's a book on the table*; *There are several books on the table*. When more than one noun follows the verb, the verb is usually singular if the first noun is singular (*There's a book and two newspapers on the table*), and plural if the first noun is plural (*There are two newspapers and a book on the table*). Less often, the verb may

agree with the notional number of a following sequence of nouns, regardless of whether they are singular or plural in form: *There are a book and a newspaper on the table*. Informally, also, there is a strong tendency to use *there's* even in sentences where the following noun is plural: *There's three books on the table*. This last usage is strongly criticized in usage manuals. (See also **here**.)

they
See **me**

this
This and *that* are both used as pronouns to refer backwards or forwards in speech or writing: compare *This gave us a new direction to follow* and *I would like to say this*. Some stylists argue that *this* should be used only when the reference is forwards, and *that* should be used only when the reference is backwards. Certainly, no one uses *that* in a forwards sense: we do not say *I would like to ask that*, referring to something which is about to be asked. But there is no basis in usage for a restriction on *this*, which is frequently used for reference in both directions.

The intensifying use of *this* or *that* before an adverb is often criticized: *It isn't that expensive*; *I didn't think it was this expensive*. These constructions are not likely to be found in formal contexts; but they are common in informal speech.

though
See **although**

through
The use of this word as a preposition in the sense 'up to and including' is standard American English, and is used in that dialect in all styles: *We shall stay Monday through Saturday*. In British English, the use of *to* or *till* is ambiguous: in *We shall stay from Monday to Saturday*, does this mean we shall leave on the Friday or the Saturday?. The only alternative is to use the phrase *up to and including*, which many people find awkward. As a result, there has been an increased use of the American construction in Britain in recent years, though not without attracting strong criticism from those who wish to keep British English as free as possible from American influence.

The use of *through* as an adjective to mean 'finished' is common, especially in informal speech, and especially in American English: *When you're through with that camera, put it back on the shelf*. The use of the word to mean 'have no further use or relationship' (*You're through!*) is also found in these contexts.

till

Till and *until* are generally interchangeable, at all stylistic levels. The choice between them is largely to do with considerations of rhythm and balance. The rhythmically 'heavier' *until* is more commonly found at the beginning of a sentence. This word also stresses the duration of time involved more than does *till*, which tends to be used more with reference to a point of time: *The light must stay on until everyone has left*, *Leave the light on till 12 o'clock*. Many people also find *till* less formal than *until*, as is reflected in the nonstandard spellings of this word as *'till* or *'til*.

to

Usage manuals reserve some of their strongest criticism for the insertion of an adverb between *to* and a verb – the so-called 'split infinitive': *I should like to formally propose an amendment*. The opposition stems from the belief, fostered by the early grammarians of English, that the infinitive construction should attempt to preserve the same kind of structural unity as it manifested in Latin, where the infinitive marker was an ending attached to the stem (as in *am-are* 'to love'). Because the infinitive form of the verb is shown by the particle *to*, therefore, it was argued that this word should stay close to the verb at all times. It is unclear why this particular grammatical issue should have attracted such strong emotions during the 19th century, but the result was an insistence on the alleged incorrectness of the split infinitive which has lasted until the present day. Although the construction is widely used in speech, and is often found in literature, the criticism has made it a sensitive issue, and it is thus often consciously avoided in formal speech or writing.

Defenders of the construction point to its ancient standing (the *Oxford English Dictionary* gives examples from the 14th century), and also argue that it can be difficult not to use a split infinitive without causing a highly unnatural style. An example is *Do you want to really help them?*, where placing *really* before *to* or after *help* leads to awkward results. Sometimes an alternative placing of the adverb produces a different meaning, as in *I have tried to deliberately stop arguing in front of the children,* where it is the stopping which is deliberate, as opposed to the trying (*I have tried deliberately ...*) or the arguing (*... to stop arguing deliberately*).

The controversy is no longer as furious as it used to be. With the reduced emphasis on traditional grammar in schools in the 1960s, public awareness of the issue has diminished, and it is out of tune with the new approaches to grammar teaching, which are less prescriptive in character. Nonetheless, many older people still express strong feelings about any use of the split infinitive construction, and letters to the BBC regularly complain about it.
(See also **try**.)

too

When preceded by *not*, *too* is often used as a form of understatement, in such sentences as *He wasn't too happy about it*, but this usage tends to be restricted to informal speech. Usage manuals would recommend *none too* or *not very* for formal contexts. Similarly, the use of *not ... too* to mean 'not very' is considered acceptable only in informal contexts: *Passage of the bill is not now considered too likely*.

towards

Towards is the prepositional form in standard British English, *toward* being used in some regional dialects: *They moved towards the town*. Both *toward* and *towards* are in standard use in American English.

try

The use of *and* following this verb is widely encountered in informal speech, especially in such established phrases as *try and get* (*Try and get some rest*) and *try and make* (*You try and make me!*). Usage manuals recommend the use of *to* instead, on the grounds that it is the usual particle for introducing an infinitive: *They should try to go home early*.

U

uninterested
See **disinterested**

unique
The absolute sense of the word *unique* to mean 'the only one of its kind' is seen as critical by purists, who insist that it should not be used in a comparative way, in careful usage, and do not allow the use of intensifying adverbs, such as *most, rather, very* or *somewhat*. On the other hand, sentences such as *That animal displays one of the most unique features of behaviour seen in Europe*, illustrate the use of the word to mean 'most unusual'. This is often encountered in informal contexts, and suggests that a less absolute sense of *unique* has emerged in modern English. *Almost* and *nearly* are not usually criticized when used with *unique*, on the grounds that no sense of degree is involved; but the boundary in meaning between *almost* and *rather* is not easy to draw, and attitudes accordingly vary on the point. The intensifying use of *quite* (*This stamp is quite unique!*) is also widely used in modern informal English, but it is unusual to encounter it in formal contexts. (See also **certain, complete, equal**.)

until
See **till**

up
See **down**

upon
See **on**

us
See **I**

use

As an auxiliary verb, *use* always occurs in the past tense, followed by *to*: *They used to go to the cinema every Friday*. In interrogative sentences, there is some variation in usage. *Used he to (go to the cinema)?* is an older construction, especially found in British English, and still sometimes employed in formal speech. The more modern and widely used form in both British and American English is *did he use(d) to*, the choice of spelling being a matter of whether the verb is seen as an auxiliary (hence *used to*) or as a main verb in it own right (hence *use to*). The latter spelling is normal in American English. A similar set of distinctions applies to the negative forms. *He usedn't to (go)* and *He used not to (go)* are the older constructions, especially found in British English, and preferred by conservative speakers. The alternative form is *didn't use(d) to (go)*, which is nowadays the dominant usage. (See also **dare**.)

V

various

This word is normally used as an adjective (*There are various possibilities*), but it is sometimes encountered as a pronoun with a collective meaning, followed by *of*: *He spoke to various of the members*. The usage has probably arisen on analogy with such forms as *several of* and *some of*, but usage manuals do not much like it, and it is generally avoided in formal contexts.

very

This word may be used to modify a past participle, when this is used as an adjective after a linking verb: *She was very cross*. When the past participle has no adjectival function, being part of a passive construction, *very* is disallowed: we cannot say *I was very kicked (by a horse)*. However, there are several cases where words have a mixture of adjective and verb functions, and the usage of *very* consequently varies. In such sentences as *He is delayed* or *They were inconvenienced*, it is possible to intensify the meaning by using *very*: *They were very inconvenienced*. However, more formal usage prefers *much*, *very much* or *greatly*, and usage manuals often criticize the use of *very* in this kind of context.

W

wait

Wait is generally used without an object: *We'll wait*. *Await* is generally used with an object: *We'll await you at the station*. When used with reference to persons and physical objects, *wait for* is the usual construction: *We were waiting for the bus*. *Await* would be extremely formal in this context: *We were awaiting the bus*. When used with reference to abstract notions, *await* is much less restricted (*We're awaiting the announcement*), and is only a little more formal than *wait for*.

-ward

The suffixes *-ward* and *-wards* are both used for the expression of direction of movement: *backward(s)*, *eastward(s)*. The forms without the *-s* are predominant in American English, and those with *-s* in British English. Certain forms allow differences of interpretation. For example, *backwards* refers to manner of motion, as well as direction – 'back first': *They pushed the car backwards down the drive*. *Backward* suggests direction only: *The car rolled backward along the drive*. Only the forms without *-s* are regularly used as adjectives (*a backward glance*), though the *-s* forms are occasionally encountered in informal speech: *She left without even a backwards glance*.

was

See **were**

we

See **I**

well

See **good**

were

In a clause expressing a hypothetical condition, *were* is the standard form to use of the verb *be*: *She spoke as if she were drunk*. *Was* is often heard in such sentences, but generally only in informal speech, and usage manuals do not recommend it. When the clause expresses a condition that is not purely hypothetical or contrary to fact, there is no problem over using *was*: *I looked to see if the way was clear*. This is also the case in indirect speech: *The manager asked whether I was going to make a complaint*. There are however several occasions when the hypothetical status of the expression is unclear, and in such cases usage is mixed: *They spoke as though everything were/was settled*. But *were* continues to be the predominant form in formal contexts. (See also **if**.)

what

The use of *what* as a relative pronoun, replacing *that*, *which* or *who*, is a noticeable characteristic of nonstandard speech, and is often picked on when satirizing such speech: *This is the latest play what I wrote*. *What ... for* is widely used in educated speech as a substitute for *why*, especially in informal contexts. Usage manuals sometimes oppose it, on the grounds that it can cause ambiguity. *What did they do it for?* could mean 'Why did they do it?' or 'How much were they paid for doing it?'. However, such cases of ambiguity are unusual. (See also **ever**, **that**, **which**.)

when

When and *where* are sometimes used in informal speech as part of a definition: *A summit conference is when/where heads of major powers come together*. Usage manuals consider this construction inelegant, and recommend its replacement in formal contexts by such constructions as *A summit conference takes place when heads of major powers come together* or *A summit conference is a meeting of heads of major powers*.

whence

This word contains the sense of 'from'. Usage manuals therefore dislike the construction *from whence*, which they consider to be an unnecessary duplication of meaning. Although the construction is quite common in informal speech, it is therefore often avoided in careful speech or writing.

whenever

See **ever**

where

Where is used with *from* to express motion from a place: *Where did they come from?* But prepositions are not required in corresponding constructions expressing motion towards: *Where did they go?* However, *to* is often used in informal speech (*Where did they go to?*) – not without criticism from usage manuals, which consider it unnecessary. (See also **ever**, **that**, **when**.)

wherever

See **ever**

whether

See **if**

which

When used as an interrogative word, *which* and *what* have different ranges of application. *Which* is generally used to suggest a choice from a number of alternatives: *Which cinema were you thinking of going to?* *What* does not involve a specific selection, and may simply express a general query: *What cinema has anything worth watching these days?* Only the first of these may be used with a following *of*: *Which of the cinemas ...?* (See also **ever**, **that**, **what**.)

while

This word may be used with reference to time (*He ate while I slept*), concession (*While I like John, I'd rather not work with him*), contrast (*The colonists imported weapons, while the Indians produced their own*) and addition (*John is French, Michael is English, while Arthur is Swedish*). This last use tends to be used only in informal speech, and has attracted strong criticism from usage manuals, which find it inelegant. Indeed, all senses of *while* other than the strictly temporal have received criticism, usually on the grounds of the potential ambiguity which can arise when temporal and non-temporal meanings are confounded, as in *He spent his youth in Ohio, while his father grew up in England*. (See also **whilst**.)

whilst

Whilst has now been generally replaced by *while* in Standard English. However, it is still used in certain literary contexts, and may still be heard amongst older British speakers, some of whom find it a more formal expression. It would be unusual to encounter it in American English. (See also **among**, **while**.)

whiskey

Whiskey is an unusual example of international spelling difference. It is the usual American English spelling, and it is found also with reference to the liquor when made in Ireland. When made in Scotland (and also in Canada), the spelling is *whisky*, and this is therefore the dominant form in British English.

who

In its use as a relative pronoun, this word has been a major source of controversy in English usage. *Who* (and *whoever*) are the standard forms to use when the pronoun functions as the subject of a clause, or follows a form of the verb *to be*: *Who's gone?*; *That's the man who left. Whom* (and *whomever*) are the forms recommended by the usage manuals when the pronoun is the object of a verb or governed by a preposition: *That is the official whom I saw*; *To whom did you speak?*. However, constructions with *whom* are generally felt to be very formal, or appropriate to writing, and they are often avoided in general conversation (*Who did you speak to?*, *That's the official who I saw*), though *whom* has to be used when governed by a preposition (*That's the official to whom Mary gave the letter*).

An interesting confusion sometimes occurs when the relative clause contains a parenthetic verb phrase, as in *We saw a man who Jim says was at the party. Who* is appropriate in this construction, according to the above rules, because it is the subject of the verb *was*; *Jim says* is parenthetic. But many people, doubtless aware of the strict grammatical rule concerning the use of *whom*, and sensing the use of a subject pronoun immediately following, in this example, opt mistakenly for the use of the object form: *He saw a man whom Jim says was at the party*.
(See also **else**, **ever**, **that**.)

whoever
See **who**

whom, whomever
See **who**

whose

This possessive form of the relative pronoun *who* can refer to both animate and inanimate entities – that is, it relates to nouns which in other circumstances would be referred to as *which*. Compare *The car which I bought ...* and *The car whose front bumper was damaged ....* There is an alternative possessive form, *of which*, but this is usually very cumbersome, and is often avoided: *The car of which the front bumper was damaged ....* (See also **else, which, who**.)

why

See **reason, what**

will

See **shall**

-wise

The use of *-wise* as a suffix for nouns, in the sense 'with reference to', is widespread in American English, and is increasingly common elsewhere. Even in American English, however, it has attracted the criticism of usage manuals, partly on account of the way in which some people use it indiscriminately (*taxwise, timewise, trainwise*, etc), and partly because many people associate it with a style of business communication which they find unpleasant. Yet the suffix continues to be used with great frequency, especially in informal speech.

woman

See **lady**

would

See **should**

Y

yet

As an adverb of time in the sense 'up to the present', this word traditionally occurs with the present perfect form of the verb: *Have they eaten yet?* However, often in informal American English, and increasingly common in British English, the form is used with the simple past tense: *Did they eat yet?*. (See also **already**.)

you

See **I**

yourself

This word, and its plural *yourselves*, is normally used in a reflexive and emphatic way: *You yourself said so!* It is not acceptable as a substitute for *you* in formal speech, though it is commonly so used informally: *I'd like to see Michael and yourself in the office later*; *How's yourself?*. Irish English seems to make more use of this substitution than any other dialect. (See also **myself**.)

-yse

See **-ize**

Glossary

This glossary gives a brief explanation of all the specialized terms used in the body of the text.

active see **passive**

adjective A type of word identifying an attribute of a noun (*a green car*).

adverb A type of word whose main function is to specify the kind of action expressed by a verb (*They walked quickly*). Other functions include acting as a sentence connector (*however*) and as an intensifier (*very*).

agreement A grammatical relationship in which the form taken by one element requires a corresponding form to be taken by another (*she* agrees with *walks*, *they* with *walk*).

analogy A change which affects a language when regular forms begin to influence irregular ones (as when young children say *mices* instead of *mice*).

animate A word (usually a noun) which refers to a living thing (*lady*, *dog*), as opposed to an object or concept (an **inanimate**, such as *stone*, *music*).

article A word which specifies whether a noun is definite or indefinite, without any further implication: the **definite article** is *the*; the **indefinite article** is *a*.

auxiliary A type of verb used along with a main verb to help express contrasts of grammar (*may, can, will, should*).

clause A unit of structure larger than a word or phrase, and often smaller than a sentence, containing such elements as subject and verb. There are two clauses in *The dog chased a cat and the cat chased a mouse*.

comparative The form of an adjective or adverb which expresses an increase in extent, relative to some standard; signalled by -*er* or *more* (*the bigger car*).

conjunction A word which connects words, phrases, and other constructions. The chief **coordinating** conjunctions are *and, or, but*; the **subordinating** conjunctions include *because, since, although*.

contraction A shortened form attached to an adjacent form (*'m* in *I'm*, short for *am*).

coordination see **conjunction**

correlative A type of construction which uses a pair of connecting words (*either...or*).

countable A type of noun which denotes separable entities, as shown by its use with such forms as *a* and *many* (*dog*, *camera*); also called a **count** noun. It is contrasted with an **uncountable** (also called a **mass**) noun, which denotes a continuous entity, as shown by its use with such forms as *much* (*information*, *music*). The contrast can be illustrated by *many dogs* and *much information*.

declarative The type of grammatical construction used in expressing a statement (*They are outside*); contrasts with **interrogative**, used in the expression of a question (*Are they outside?*).

elliptical A type of sentence where an element or elements have been omitted, but which are understood from the context (*To town*, as a response to *Where are you going?*).

etymology The study of the origins and history of the form and meaning of words.

generic A word or sentence which refers to a class of entities (*the Chinese*, *the poor*).

gerund A word derived from a verb and used as a noun, especially as found in Latin grammar, or in grammars based on Latin (*Smoking is bad for you*).

impersonal A type of construction which lacks a personal or animate agent (*It's raining*, *The cup was broken*).

inanimate see **animate**

indirect question A type of question in which the speaker's words are made subordinate to a verb of 'saying' (*She asked whether it was time to go*).

infinitive The basic form of the verb, used without any ending, and often preceded by the particle *to* (*to go*, *sit*). The form without *to* is sometimes called the 'bare' infinitive.

inflection An ending which signals a grammatical relationship, such as plural, past tense, or possession (*-s*, *-ed*).

intensifier A word or phrase which adds force or emphasis (*very*, *quite*).

interrogative see **declarative**

intonation The use of pitch movement to express contrasts of meaning in speech.

linking verb A type of verb whose main role is to link other elements of the clause, most commonly forms of *be* (*She is happy*).

mass see **countable**

Glossary

modify To stand in a subordinate relation to, as when an adjective is said to 'modify' a noun (*the red chair*).

negative A form which expresses the denial or contradiction of some or all of the meaning of a sentence, typically *not* or *no*. A sentence which lacks a marker of negation is a **positive** sentence.

non-restrictive see **restrictive**

noun A type of word with a naming function, typically showing contrasts of number and countability, and capable of acting as the subject or object of a clause (*cow*, *music*).

number The grammatical category which expresses such contrasts as singular vs plural.

object The element in a clause which usually follows the verb, and typically expresses the result of an action (*the ball* in *James kicked the ball*); also called the **direct object**.

objective The form taken by some pronouns when it occurs as the object of a verb or after a preposition (*John saw me*, *The woman gave the book to her*). When these pronouns occur as subject, they are said to be in the **subjective** form.

participle A word derived from a verb and used as an adjective (*a smiling face*, *a parked car*).

passive A type of relationship between the subject and object of a verb, expressing an action which affects the subject (*The cat was chased by the dog*); contrasts with the **active** relationship of *The dog chased the cat*.

perfect A form of the verb typically expressing a past action which has present relevance, such as the **present perfect** use of *have* (*It has arrived*).

person A grammatical form which refers to the speaker (the 'first person'), addressee (the 'second person') or others involved in the interaction (the 'third person(s)'); typically expressed by pronouns and verbs.

phrase A group of words forming a grammatical unit smaller than a clause. Phrases include **noun phrases** (*the large house*) and **verb phrases** (*has been running*).

plural see **singular**

positive see **negative**

possessive A type of word or ending which indicates possession (*my*, *'s*).

preposition A part of speech which governs and usually precedes nouns, pronouns, and certain other forms, expressing such notions as time, location, or manner (*in*, *onto*, *by*).

present perfect see **perfect**

pronoun A part of speech which can substitute for a noun or noun phrase (*I*, *she*, etc).

restrictive A modifying word or phrase which is an essential part of the identity of another element (*my uncle who's abroad has written to me*); contrasts with **nonrestrictive**, where the modification is not essential, and could be omitted without loss to the basic meaning of the sentence (*My uncle, who's abroad, has written to me*).

singular A form which typically expresses 'one of' in number; contrasted with **plural**, which typically expresses 'more than one' in number (*car* vs *cars*; *It is* vs *they are*).

stem The part of a word to which endings are attached (*carpet – s*).

stress The degree of force with which a syllable is uttered. A **stressed** syllable, uttered with relatively strong force, is distinguished from an **unstressed** syllable, uttered with relatively weak force. In this book, stressed syllables are indicated by ' (*ba'nana*, *'package*).

subject The element in a clause about which something is stated in the predicate; typically, the 'doer' of the action, preceding the verb (*The girl* in *The girl drove the car*).

subjective see **objective**

subordination see **conjunction**

superlative The extreme degree of comparison expressed by an adjective or adverb; signalled by *-est* or *most* (*the largest portion*).

tense A change in the form of a verb to mark the time at which an action takes place (present tense *walk*, past tense *walked*).

transitive A type of verb which can take a direct object (*kick*); contrasts with **intransitive**, where the verb cannot take an object (*go*).

uncountable see **countable**

unstressed see **stress**

verb A type of word typically used to express an action, event, or state, and displaying tense and other contrasts (*know*, *kick*).